The A-Z
of Self-Employment

The A-Z
of Self-
Employment

SIDNEY BLOCH

SECOND EDITION

ASHFORD, BUCHAN & ENRIGHT, PUBLISHERS

First published in 1989 by Buchan & Enright, Publishers

This edition published by Ashford, Buchan & Enright, Publishers
31 Bridge Street, Leatherhead, Surrey KT22 8BN

British Library Cataloguing in Publication Data

Bloch, Sidney, 1924-1990
The A-Z of self-employment — Manuals
I. Title
658' .041'0941

ISBN 1 85253 258 0

Typeset by Priory Publications, Haywards Heath
Printed in Great Britain by FotoDirect Ltd., Brighton

CONTENTS

CONTENTS

Your Own Agencies

CONTENTS

Commission Agencies

Miscellaneous

Postscript

Introduction

NOW START YOUR OWN BUSINESS

Years ago, Somerset Maugham wrote *The Verger,* a success story about an intelligent, middle-aged man who was sacked by the elders of his church. It turned out to be the best thing that ever happened to him.

Today, with international trade agreements, computers and industrial modernisation, there are countless different reasons why numerous competent managers, miners, factory workers, clerks, labourers, artisans, scientists and professional men and women make up our large battalions of unemployed. Sadly, the side-effect of commercial progress and changing needs is increased unemployment. In consequence, countless able people continue to find it difficult or impossible to obtain permanent employment. Worst of all is that there are those prepared to accept this situation and others compelled to do so. What is too often overlooked, however, is the fact that there are hundreds of thousands of men and women in a very special category. Blessed with intelligence, drive and initiative, they only need an idea and one or two practical examples to get them thinking positively and moving forward again. These are the people for whom this book is written. It does not offer an easy answer for all the unemployed, but it is to be hoped that it will assist many — particularly those men and women who have had their confidence shaken, or the many others seeking to create a new life which offers a challenge, an interest and the opportunity to earn a realistic income. This is the large group of people who rightly refuse to accept that they are unemployable. These are the intelligent people who are not prepared to believe that they are unable to earn a good living. They know only too well that all too often they are the innocent victims of circumstance or mismanagement.

An interesting example is Arnold Dalton, a storeman employed by a public company for twenty-five years. At the age of fifty-two, computerisation made him redundant. He received a few thousand pounds, a reduced pension and a fairly new Ford car. Recovering from the shock of finding himself unemployed, he applied to over two hundred large and small companies for a job. The majority did not even bother to reply, and not one of those who did invited him to an interview. Reluctantly, Arnold faced the reality that companies seeking a storeman were not interested in someone in his age group. No doubt some considered him over the hill, and others reckoned that it would be too expensive to fund his pension. Suddenly, he felt shattered by the thought that, without even being seen, he had been judged a has-been. Industry, in its wisdom, had decided that he was no longer a storeman but a statistic. He was just another one of so many able people who might well remain out of work for the rest of their lives. For all his distress and confusion, he made a resolution that he was determined to keep: he was simply not going to accept the verdict or the sentence. Come what may, he, Arnold Dalton, was going to prove that he could still make it. If not as a storeman then as something else, but he was not going to be listed among the unemployed for long. 'I have the wrong stomach and the wrong chemistry,' he told himself. Shortly afterwards he sat down and wrote out his problem in detail. Slowly, he read it through several times. Gradually, a plan emerged. Not just an idea but a course of action that suited his temperament and renewed his self-confidence. He decided that the first step was to sell his Ford and with the proceeds buy a well-maintained Jaguar that was four years older. From that day he became a mini-cab driver. At first sight there seems to be nothing especially original about his decision, but this was only the beginning. Reading through his notes, he realised that his thinking had travelled along the following lines.

1. Regardless of what anyone else thinks, I believe that because I am fit, honest and competent, I am still able to find myself a worthwhile occupation.
2. There are no jobs available for those in my age group which require my particular experience. This is the first fact that I have to accept and live with. From now on I will not think of myself as a storeman.
3. Nobody has offered me a job and I have no reason to believe that anyone will. I must accept that I am on my own. Only I can create a new future for myself.
4. Somehow, I must find work which will bring me into contact with people who might give me an idea of the kind of opportunity which I need.
5. Those who use mini-cabs fall into two categories: people who simply need private transport from time to time, and those who can afford the luxury of being driven in comfort but do not wish to carry the permanent overhead of a chauffeur.

6. The vast majority of mini-cab drivers own less expensive cars. If I run a prestige motor car, I am likely to meet the more affluent customer. In that way I stand a reasonable chance of having the opportunity to speak to a number of influential business men. It will then be up to me to make my case for my future.

Mini-cabbing gave Arnold a reasonable income largely because he was prepared to work long hours. He stayed cheerful and kept his dreams to himself. Four months later, fortune smiled on him. A manufacturer whom he had taken on a number of long journeys casually confided that he was looking for a reliable man with whom to start a specialised import and export business. Arnold struck gold. Today, he can write his own success story. His erstwhile colleagues from his old company are mostly still unemployed. Of course it is not suggested that everyone with a driving licence and no job should become a mini-cab driver, but his thinking process must be worth emulating. This book is for those who want to think this way but simply need a few guidelines.

For anyone to obtain the maximum benefits with the minimum delay it is absolutely essential that he or she accepts two basic conditions. The first is that before reading any further you make up your mind to stop thinking of yourself as unemployed. From this moment you are someone who is between being employed and starting your own business. Don't be embarrassed because you are drawing unemployment benefit. It is not a hand-out, it is not charity, it is a right for which you have paid. You are probably just drawing back part of all the money you have paid in over the years. The second condition is that you are genuinely prepared to embark on a new life regardless of whether it relates to your qualifications, your previous employment or to your social circle.

The verger who left his church employers did not look for another church. He recognised an opportunity to start a little business with a modest amount of capital. Eventually, he became a very comfortable man. This book cannot guarantee that every reader will do as well as quickly; it is to be hoped, however, that there will be many who will, and many others who will ultimately benefit from the thought processes and the ideas which are developed. The businesses covered in this book are a selection from many possibilities. Even if none appeals completely to every reader, they are presented in the hope that they will spawn ideas along similar lines.

The time has now arrived to be thinking positively. Remember you are only going to continue reading for one reason: you firmly believe that you have the intelligence and the determination to start a small business and to stick at it until it works profitably. I hope that, as you turn the page, you will be taking your first step in creating a new, stimulating and profitable career for yourself.

Sidney Bloch

Sidney Bloch, my husband and author of this book, was one of seven children in a family he described as being long on spiritual assets and short on cash.

Leaving school at fourteen, he was a dispatch rider in the London Fire Brigade during the Blitz. At seventeen he volunteered for the Army.

Five years later, on his demobilization, he 'went into insurance', a virtually self educated young man, operating from a reference library and a public telephone box. His business prospered and he became chairman of a broking and underwriting group at Lloyd's, subsequently leaving the City to form his own international financial consultancy.

Sadly, Sidney died in October 1990, the last years of his life spent in the shadow of an illness he knew to be incurable. This never stifled his enthusiasm and determination and he continued to dedicate considerable time and energy to his writing, his business activities and, especially, to his work in the field of welfare.

He was chairman of two major voluntary agencies and, at the time of his death, was deeply involved in the establishment of an All-Party Parliamentary Group on Race and Community, designed to improve the status of ethnic and racial minorities.

His family, to which he was devoted, his friends and his business colleagues, remember Sidney as a man who never did anything half-heartedly and who believed that life had to be spent 'in top gear'. He had an innovative, almost superactive mind, a ready wit and great compassion for those less fortunate than himself. He never hesitated to speak out where he saw injustice and was ever ready to listen and to offer wise and constructive advice.

I hope that this book will continue to inspire all those who plan to launch a small business. Their success will be the tribute he would have valued most.

Lilian Bloch

1

THINKING
AND
OBSERVING

This illustration is of a typical suburban street. The business names have been chosen for easy recognition and not in any way to indicate or to reflect the business philosophy or style of their owners. The comments on the pages that follow are made purely to emphasise the differences between the casual and the conscientious observer.

MAIN STREET

				POWER STREET			

P BUILDING SOC
GREETINGS CARDS
DOLCIS
P SAINSBURY
ELECTRICITY Co
P HALFORDS
WOOLWORTH
P JEWELLER
P TO LET
DIXONS
LILLEY & SKINNER
P NAT WEST
NEXT

POWER STREET

W. H. SMITH
MARKS & SPENCER   P
BARCLAYS   P
BRITISH HOME STORES
BOOTS
CHINACRAFT
ESTATE AGENTS   P
TESCO
TRAVEL AGENCY   P

P Parking space

15

Looking for ideas

Understandably, the vast majority of people entering this suburban shopping precinct would be there for one of two purposes. Either to make a bee-line for a particular store or office, or simply to indulge in casual window shopping. The man with the entrepreneurial mind, looking for ideas for a new business, on the other hand, would allocate plenty of time just to stand and stare and observe. He would know that his prime purpose in being there is to study everything in sight, carefully appraise the situation and try to recognise opportunities or products which could help him establish or enhance his own business. He would endeavour to keep his eyes and his mind completely open. In this way ideas which might not help him directly could register and possibly spin off one that would be worth developing. He would examine the location, note significant landmarks, look into shop windows and into the shops themselves. He would study the customers, mentally categorise their age-groups and try to recognise their priorities.

Investing time

Above all, he would not be in a hurry. He would be conscious of being a man investing time, his most precious asset. He would be determined that, in one way or another, he is going to make a profit from this exercise or a similar one.

One might well imagine our entrepreneur, aware of the importance of keeping accurate records, dictating into a small tape-recorder the following account of his visit for future reference.

The record starts here

Today is Wednesday, 16th October. It is 9 a.m., and it is a bright morning. I am standing at the corner of Main Street and Power Street near the building society. Looking down Main Street, I can see several large office blocks standing beyond some fifty or sixty small shops. About eight of them appear to be to let. At the end of the shopping parade is a large garage opposite a post office. A string of new shops is being built along the other side of Main Street. Power Street is a very wide precinct. It is quiet. More than half the shops are still closed.

Thoughts about the high street

There are few shoppers, most of whom look like office workers. They are making straight for Marks & Spencer, Tesco or Sainsbury's. The greetings-card shop seems incongruous, sited as it is among tenants of such high standing. Maybe it has a long lease at a low rent or a surprisingly high turnover — despite the fact that Boots, British Home Stores, W.H. Smith and Woolworth's all sell cards. If the lease could be purchased, it would enable Dolcis to expand. Maybe one could also acquire the lease of Dolcis and provide a larger shop for a new tenant, like Burtons or Mothercare. There are no up-market clothing stores apart from Next. I have now walked down the entire shopping parade for the first time.

Questions without answers

It is now 9.45, and most of the shops are open. It seems strange that there is a shop to let. Maybe Dixons have taken it but have decided to defer expansion until after Christmas.... Can never understand why a company with a monopoly like the Electricity Company has to occupy a prime position in so many high streets.... National Westminster has a brighter appearance than Barclays in spite of the latter being in a better trading position.... The estate agency must have a good business to occupy offices of that size — I wonder how much space they actually use.... Boots could make more of its window dressing, particularly as they have become so much a general store rather than just a pharmacy.... I have just walked round Woolworths and feel they could do better. Simply because they sell lower-priced goods does not seem a good reason for some of their counters to appear less imaginative than those of Marks & Spencer and British Home Stores. The toy section seems too small to be profitable.

Opening hours

It is 10.15. There are still not many people around. Only a handful have visited the banks. Would it be better if they opened an hour later and stayed open an hour longer? Expect it would cause trouble with the unions.... There seem to be more people in Sainsbury's than in Tesco. I wonder why.... Halfords is also fairly empty. It is an interesting shop with hundreds of gadgets but not many staff. Perhaps they have more later in the day.... There is nowhere in the precinct to have a coffee. Would it pay Woolworths to build a really nice coffee bar at the rear of the store in order to attract a different class of customer? Probably no profit in suggesting the idea to them. Somewhere, I remember hearing that most large companies never buy ideas; they only steal them. I wonder if they would do better if they reversed their priorities?... Lilley and Skinner have barely had a customer.... A few mothers with babies in prams are arriving. Most leave the prams outside the shops and carry the babies with them.

Danger, window-cleaner

It is 11.00. A window-cleaner has started cleaning the windows of one of the stores. Someone could easily collide with his ladder. Crazy time to start. His ladder is too short. I wonder what the odds are of his causing an accident.... It would seem worthwhile wandering round the perimeter before taking a tour round the shops themselves.

Parking space is good for business

It is midday and not very warm. I have walked round the rear of the shops. Only Sainsbury's and M&S have any real parking areas. This no doubt accounts for the larger number of customers they enjoy. Nine of the tenants have wasted space at the rear. Most do not require loading bays and their premises have not been extended. I estimate that there is around 3,000 square feet of unused space highly suitable for parking. Delivery vans waste a great deal of time manoeuvring their vehicles and thereby blocking private cars. It could be something for the shopkeepers' association to look into in their own interest....

Rubbish and security

There is a fair amount of rubbish about, indicating that either it is not cleared daily or it is not adequately supervised.... Three of the shops have alarm boxes almost hanging off their outside walls. They must either be fakes or faulty.

It is 1.15 p.m. The shopping precinct is becoming a busy thoroughfare. Most of the shoppers are aged between sixteen and fifty, but there is a good sprinkling of the elderly.... The window-cleaner has finished and gone away. He either has only one customer or comes several times a week....

No real selling staff

Walking round the stores, it is apparent that the majority have staff who serve their customers politely. None appear to have sales personnel who actually sell. One wonders if they actually have any training. Would it be worthwhile for stores to encourage every counter-employee to mention another product to each customer?

Sales training

Would it improve sales if every morning the manager or supervisor gave each assistant a 'line' like 'Have you looked at our shirt department today?' or 'Have you seen our perfume counter?'...? One or two of the stores attract relatively few customers while others could well do with more space.... Both banks now have queues. One is obviously too small for the trade, and the other is only using three out of its five counters.... M&S and BHS must have hundreds of suppliers and manufacturers. The small man would hardly be able to compete in supplying the big stores. Maybe there is more scope for business with one or more of the suppliers. Anyone who supplies these big stores must have a constant need for all sorts of goods. They should be able to pay promptly....

Marks & Spencer, Bankers

Could M&S enter the banking field? They must have enough customers and suppliers to consider the service industry. They don't need me to tell them.... My mind keeps coming back to suppliers, their constant need for the most modern machinery, their overheads and their thin profit margins....

A tatty window

The estate agents' has in its window an attractive display of expensive houses, but the price cards look tatty. Wonder why they don't employ an interior decorator to provide a complementary service to buyers. Strange that estate agents never seem to have strong links with builders and decorators. There should be scope in the concept.... Prams are now very much in evidence.

Careless mothers

Some thoughtless mothers actually leave their babies unattended.... I have been here over four hours and have just seen my first policeman.

Will take one more slow stroll up and down the precinct in case I have missed something obvious. The greetings-card shop has a photocopying machine for the public. Would hardly have thought it worthwhile.... Halfords have an enormous selection of car accessories and screwdrivers.... Chinacraft's windows almost invite customers into the shop....

Travel agency window has a message

The comparatively large window of the travel agency is cluttered up with brochures in no special order. That window is trying to tell me something.... Looking back up Power Street, I can see the policeman holding the handles of two unattended occupied prams ....

Our entrepreneur would now return home, play his recording two or three times, and write down his conclusions as follows:

The feedback

Conclusions

1. Trade in the complex would not be effected by opening time being changed to 10 a.m.
2. The banking service is not efficient.
3. Several shops offer scope for development at rear. Lack of supervision could well create a fire hazard.
4. Halfords worth a longer visit to list unusual gadgets which might be produced more cheaply or marketed differently.
5. List manufacturers of different goods at M&S and BHS, — e.g. cotton, wool, paper, food — for reference if ever thinking of starting a small business supplying suppliers.

Writing out notes to think about

6. Would it be possible to arrange a window-cleaning contract for all the tenants? One that finished before the shops opened.
7. No sandwich bar for passing customers or for the hundreds of local staff.
8. Look at price cards in windows of other estate agents. Might be worth checking the rest of their stationery.
9. Obtain catalogues from major toy shops and check any items suitable for Woolworths.
10. Security for prams — locks and labels. Wonder if anyone has thought of pram alarms.
11. BHS has the best lampshade selection.
12. The selection at the greetings-card shop was more colourful but more expensive than in other stores.
13. Few of the sales-staff showed any initiative.
14. The travel agency was trying to tell me something.
15. The precinct would be well served by a few benches for elderly shoppers.
16. Space at the rear could provide additional parking and possibly a pram park.

Stupid ideas can also be valuable

This exercise would be repeated a number of times. Notes on prices, design and quality would prove useful when considering which business to start. It should be remembered that what at first might appear an irrelevant or even stupid idea could well lead you to a more practical one.

The Henry Ford story

Henry Ford was fond of relating the story of a man who, in the 1930s, believed there was money to be made in changing the shape of the nuts which secured car wheels. For months he made coloured sketches in the hope that he would eventually create a new image for nuts.

Suddenly, scribbling away, the idea occurred to him that a large centre nut could well do the job of the usual four. He patented it and tried to sell the idea to a major American car manufacturer. They were certainly interested. In no time a group of American car manufacturers paid him $1,000,000 for the patent — it was a cheap price for them to pay to enable them to maintain their profits by continuing to produce sixteen nuts per car instead of four. The tale might be apocryphal but it does illustrate that no idea should be dismissed out of hand.

Success story

Apart from determination and initiative, the ability to recognise opportunities has probably been the greatest single factor that has helped enterprising men to launch fresh businesses. The example quoted above will be referred to several times throughout this book. Suffice it to say that the entrepreneur quoted actually exists. He revisited the precinct on four more occasions, each time checking out and enlarging on the notes which he had made. Suddenly, he realised what it was that the window in the travel agency was trying to tell him. It represented a missed opportunity.

Happy ending

Every single customer who called at that office was interested in travelling somewhere, and yet the window was only filled with brochures. It was not long before the entrepreneur was busy building a profitable business selling all sizes of luggage to travel agents.

Women more observant

Many men and women have recognised business opportunities by training themselves to be more observant. Without generalising, women often have a natural tendency in this area, frequently excelling in the types of intelligence test that require spotting 'gaps and misfits'.

2

DECIDING ON A BUSINESS

When one is hungry

It has always been alleged that the vast majority of men and women who started life with little or no capital were driven into business by sheer necessity. This is well illustrated by the story of a hungry young salesman who, when asked by a potential customer for the main reason for his call, replied, 'One wife and three children.' When men like Montague Burton began making trousers, and John Cohen piled up groceries at the back of a lorry, and Charles Forte sold sandwiches, they were not consciously thinking of careers or of making millions. Like others before and since, most were concerned with making enough to keep body and soul together. Had someone offered any of these men a secure job, the chances are that we would never have heard of them. The fact remains that nearly all the successful men and women who started from humble origins were motivated by a desperate desire to enjoy three meals a day in a home with its own bathroom. Ambitions and aspirations came much later.

Worried or bored

Most of those hoping to derive some benefit from this book will not actually be hungry. Many will have known better times, some will be worried for their future and others will possibly be bored by frustration or inactivity.

Desire for a lifestyle

More than likely, they will have at least two things in common: a desire to continue or re-establish a given lifestyle, and a wish to be usefully occupied. Enthusiastic readers must find some time to take stock of opportunities and to make a conscious decision of what they would like to do, before stepping into a new career. Hopefully, the guidelines detailed in the following chapters will help many to avoid the pitfalls so often suffered by those obliged to learn entirely from their own mistakes.

Impatience and caution

This book has really been written for the impatient enthusiast who cannot wait to get up and get started. But a word of caution is warranted at this stage. Anyone seriously contemplating a long-term commitment should give careful thought to every aspect of it. Furthermore, if there are practical alternatives, they too should be studied with equal attention. Regrets are suffered mostly by people who give insufficient thought to matters of the greatest importance. The following checklist has been prepared to prevent this happening to you.

Just for once take it slowly

It is worth pondering over it before getting down to the real business of helping yourself carve out a new career. This is the only time when it will be recommended that you take things slowly.

Think of the problems

* Do you have the determination to make a real effort to establish a small business?
* Do you realise that every business, however small, will sometimes bring disappointment?
* Have you decided whether you would be as happy working outdoors as indoors?
* Do you realise that there is absolutely no point in starting certain businesses if a physical disability is likely to prevent you from continuing? (Bad backs or weak chests don't usually go away.)
* Have you decided on the minimum amount which you will want your new business to earn for you after you have paid all your overheads?
Have you considered the maximum amount you can honestly afford to put into any business?
* Do you realise that a new business will, more often than not, demand longer hours and impose far more strain than any normal job?
* Do you realise that starting a business is not only exciting and challenging, it is also lonely?
* Will you be pleased to tell your wife/husband and family about your new business and its progress?

Drive and hard work, not luck

* Do you appreciate that this book is about starting little businesses and not about little people? Every reader who launches a new venture, however small its beginning, is going to need drive, initiative and determination together with a willingness to work really hard for long periods.

From this moment the chapters are written for people who have decided that they want a new challenge because they have what it takes to meet it. The practical suggestions made in the following pages should certainly assist a large number of people to start the businesses described. Even more will perhaps apply the same principles to launching other, different, small enterprises, of which there are many. The day before this chapter was written, a Sussex newspaper reported an excellent example of initiative. When a local hairdressing salon closed down, an experienced hairdresser found herself without a job, and was unable to find another within eight miles of her home. Not having the capital to rent premises, she started offering a local home hairdressing service. A year later she is too busy to take on any more business clients. In addition, she also supplies many of her customers with cosmetics and small gifts.

Before moving forward, there are two very important matters to take into account. The first is that, since 1982, the Government Enterprise Allowance Scheme encourages unemployed people to start their own businesses.

£40 a week for trying

Subject to a few formalities, it grants £40 a week for up to a year to anyone with even a simple idea which stands a good chance of succeeding. The full details are available from any Job Centre. These allowances are not charity: they have proved an excellent investment for the Government, and for more than 500,000 people who have taken advantage of the scheme.

Consideration should also be given to effecting a sickness and accident insurance policy. This would provide you with an income in the event of a physical disability preventing you from running your business. It is not a cheap policy, so do bear the following in mind:

1. If your spouse or partner is able to keep the business running for a time, there may not be too great an urgency to effect such a policy until you are sure you can afford it.
2. These policies are much cheaper if you are prepared not to claim for a period. Initially, you may decide only to provide benefits if you are totally disabled for a period longer than three months. Whatever you decide, do not

spend a lot of money on insurance until you are quite sure your business idea is working.

As you read on, remember that you are now fully employed in preparing the foundation for your own constructive and profitable future.

3

PROFESSIONAL ASSISTANCE

This chapter might just as well come right at the end of the book. The decision to bring it in so early is to assure you that, at this stage, your only priority is to decide on the business which you wish to start.

The time for advisers

In the areas of small one-man businesses, lawyers and accountants are rarely trained to recognise talent outside their own professions or to advise people how or why they should start a particular small business. They are useful and even essential to all business men at certain times but they can be dismissed from your thoughts for the moment. They will not be forgotten.

A good free adviser

The only person to bear in mind right now is your bank manager. Whatever you decide to do, he will probably be the first outsider you will speak to about your new business. He knows your account, and even if you've never met him, he's probably got a pretty good idea about your lifestyle. Bank managers are trained to recognise such things from the cheques and paying-in slips of their customers. They are also trained to honour confidences.

Knowledge on call

In addition, even though the bank manager is constantly under pressure from his head office to make more money for his branch, he does not usually charge for his time at the initial stages. That is worth bearing in mind.

Apart from his own experience, he has a mine of useful information available to him. Unlike the average accountant or solicitor, he also has a wealth of knowledge on call from his area and head offices. Starting a business is the best time to find out exactly how helpful your bank manager can be. He is the first man to speak to when you are ready to make your decision, and certainly before you commit yourself to more than a modest amount of capital. He is also a useful man to use as a sounding board and to help you decide which solicitor, accountant or insurance broker to consult. Never feel hesitant in calling on him.

His business is built on the goodwill of people like you. His advice is often more reliable than that of the big business man who might well be out of touch with the ins and outs of starting a modest enterprise.

Remember, banks need you as much as you need them

If, for any reason, you do not have confidence in your bank manager, or if you find him inattentive, patronising or flippant, do not hesitate to change your bank.

Remember, banks are not benevolent societies. They impose charges wherever they can get away with it. They need new customers, not just for normal banking business but for all the fringe benefits like credit cards, travellers' cheques, insurance and the many other services which they offer. Their major stocks in trade, as far as you are concerned, are courtesy and advice. Wherever you keep your bank account or your overdraft, you are entitled to both.

Chapter 34, 'Wealth Warnings', on page 175, is particularly relevant. It comes nearer the end of the book, rather than the beginning, so that it should not be forgotten by those impatient to get started.

4

AIDS
TO
STARTING

Start now with confidence

The placing of this chapter, might, like the previous one, surprise some people, but there is a purpose behind it. When reading of the numerous opportunities that fill this book, there could be those who nurture doubts simply because they would not be sure how to begin. Such people should be assured that, as far as possible, every stage, in every business listed, will be covered to enable those interested to move into gear with confidence and without any reservations.

Unless you have actually been in business or are involved in politics, communal societies or social clubs, you are unlikely to be very well known outside your immediate social circle.

Personal references

This is not unusual. It probably applies to more than ninety-five per cent of the entire population, including engineers, commercial accountants, analysts, factory foremen, railway staff, school teachers and most professional men and women. The only real problem that this creates when starting a business is one of credibility. Understandably, people like to know who they are dealing with, particularly if services of a personal nature are being offered.

Old employers

Many of you may not want to go back to your old employers for a reference. It is an attitude that is quite understandable for a number of good reasons. First, having lost a job or been made redundant, privacy becomes very precious indeed and many of us are reluctant to advertise our predicament. One simply does not wish to share confidences with those who have dispensed with one's services, whether their reasons were understandable or not. Secondly, the only reference available from this source may well lack the positive recommendation that is needed. Still, it should not be ignored. It could prove useful if only to confirm that you were actually employed for some time and that your reasons for leaving do not reflect on your character.

Others

Fortunately, there are often other, less obvious, people from whom good references might be obtained. If it is not too long since you left school and your old headmaster or headmistress is likely to remember you, drop them a note on the following lines:

Getting letters right

Dear Mr/Mrs Briggs,
Since I left your school I have been employed as a _____ with XYZ Ltd. It was a good job until I was made redundant when the company was taken over. It now occurs to me that this could be an ideal opportunity for me to start my own small business. Although it is some time since we last met I would be most grateful if I might include your name among my referees.
Better still would be if you could let me have a reference addressed 'To Whom It May Concern'.
Of course I would be happy to call on you if you would prefer to discuss it first.
With kindest regards,
Yours sincerely,

(Name in full)

Then write a similar letter to your doctor, and enclose stamped self-addressed envelopes in each. Your third application for a reference should be made to your bank manager, who will reply without your having to pay for the stamp.

Keep copies

When you receive the references, the first thing to do is to have a few photocopies made so that the originals can be kept looking like originals. Most public libraries have photocopiers for the convenience of the public, and librarians invariably have plenty of change too. The charges are always modest, and, as the machines are self-operated, there is no fear of anyone reading your private mail.

Your Member of Parliament loves to be wanted

The next step is to write a special letter to your Member of Parliament. It makes no difference which party he represents or whether you have ever seen him. He will certainly reply, if only because you live in his constituency, you are a voter and, above all, he wants to maintain or create a reputation for being polite, understanding and concerned. Something along the following lines should produce the right answer. Do remember to check the spelling of his name and whether or not he has any degrees or decorations. Most people, not just MPs, love to see them on envelopes, if only to impress the postman.

Flattery is always welcome

George Briggsworthy, Esq., MP, BA (Hons),
House of Commons, London SW1 0AA.

Dear Mr Briggsworthy,
As a member of your constituency, I am prompted to write to you for a small favour. Your well-known concern for the unemployed has long meant a great deal to many like myself. Unfortunately, I was among those made redundant *(or whatever)* when XYZ Ltd was taken over *(or when the Government made cut-backs at the ZKO plant, etc.)*.
In an effort to turn a misfortune into an opportunity I feel this could well be an excellent time for me to start a small business. Appreciating that I may well require suitable references, I have obtained a number, copies of which I enclose. It would be most helpful if you could let me have a note 'To Whom It May Concern' confirming that you have seen them and indicating your own attitude to the encouragement of unemployed persons like myself to take initiative.
Of course it would be perfectly in order for you to make contact with the other referees should you wish to do so.
Yours sincerely,

(Full name)

Preserve your own reputation

Always acknowledge a reference. You never know when you might need another, and in any case a reputation for politeness can never do any harm. This bunch of references should be quite sufficient for all normal purposes but it is always worthwhile to obtain others from people of standing. You may never need all the references that you can get, but it could be useful to have some extra ones on your file. They are part of your stock in trade until you are well established.

Vicars and football club managers

Other useful referees might include your vicar, the chairman of the local football club, the manager of the building society where you obtained your mortgage, the solicitor you used when you bought your house, and anyone else who can vouch for your ability or your integrity. There are many companies, small and large, who keep albums of letters from satisfied customers and well-wishing suppliers. It could be useful for you to do the same with your references.

5

VALUING
YOUR
TIME

Time is money

Putting a price on your time is unnecessary if you are simply looking for a hobby or something interesting to help you pass the time. But a business is not in this category. It is absolutely essential that anyone considering a new venture should endeavour to evaluate its financial potential.

There is no mileage in becoming enthusiastic about any business or service unless one is convinced that it has the potential to produce the minimum income or profit which one would find adequate.

How much do you need?

A modest example would be a man prepared to work fifty hours a week in the hope of earning at least £200. In order to allow for travelling time, gaps in his work programme and, if he is working outside, weather conditions, it would be necessary for him to charge his time out at £5 per hour. This assumes that he is working eight hours a day, five days a week. Of course if the work requires special skills then the established rate needs to be ascertained. It is then up to the individual to decide whether or not he wishes to increase his hourly rate or remain competitive.

Spin-offs and no spin-offs

It is particularly important to put a value to your time in those instances where there are no possible spin-off benefits. A contract to cut public hedges for a local authority, for example, is unlikely to produce additional money-making opportunities. There are, however, other areas which can offer scope for much greater enterprise — for example, car-valeting and household services, as elaborated in Chapters 18 and 24.

Everybody pays for good value

Rates of pay, fees, commissions and profits will be covered throughout the book. The point that is being emphasised here is that you should only consider a particular business once you are satisfied that it can give you a fair return for your time, your effort or your investment. No business man ever became successful by operating like a casual labourer.

Never sell yourself cheap

Contrary to popular opinion, most people are prepared to pay a fair price for goods and reliable services. In the latter case, appearance, courtesy and a reputation for doing a good job are far more likely to get you well established than selling yourself too cheaply.

These days, those who offer poor work and indifferent attitudes in an effort to make easy money provide great opportunities for competitors.

Good work pays best

Those who conscientiously and politely carry out their services efficiently should feel confident in charging fair rates for their labour. Even bargain-hunters and skinflints know that a good man is worthy of his hire.

One more very important point. Make your calculations on a normal working week, and not on the long hours that you may be prepared to devote to your business. Failure to do this means that you are sharing your hard-earned profit with your customers.

Overtime is your real profit

Of course, the ideal cannot always be achieved but, in principle, the hourly rate which you decide is right for the job should not take into account your overtime — that should be your real profit.

6

CONVERSATION STOPPERS

Whether you are endeavouring to sell a service or a product, you will be bound to come up against potential customers who try and stop you in your tracks. Some will be impatient because they have other matters on their minds, and others will doubt the value of whatever it is you want to sell them.

Do not be disheartened

Then there is the largest group who are either poor listeners or believe they know it all. The art of the game is not to be disheartened or put off by these people. The following short list of rebuffs and suggested answers might be worth memorising. It is not just because you could find them useful, but also to help you appreciate and be prepared for discouraging receptions and to take them in your stride.

Customer: I'm sorry I'm busy.
You (smile and don't be thrown): Of course, I understand. I'd be pleased to call again when it's more convenient. I'm really sure you will be interested in what I have to say.
Customer: Come in next time you're passing.
You: I'd like to do that. When is the best time of the day for you? *(This throws the ball right back to the customer. He is obliged to give you a helpful answer or, alternatively, make it plain that you are wasting your time.)*
Customer: We have our regular suppliers.
You: I'm sure you do. But my business is to compete with them to give our customers a more competitive price/quotation or service.
Customer: I would probably be wasting your time.
You: That's a chance I'd like to take. My business is being built on people like you who are prepared to listen.
Customer: I can't listen now, I'm short-staffed.

You (This is not always a rebuff. It could be a golden opportunity): Is there any way I can help?

Be helpful where possible

(This answer, given years ago by an enthusiastic insurance salesman, was responsible for his obtaining one of the largest accounts in his career. He offered to assist a director of what was then a small mail-order company to open more than two thousand replies to an advertisement. Subsequently, he helped with the parcels and their dispatch. Two major factors contributed to his success. He took on a job he knew he could handle and he was prepared to invest the time to create goodwill.)

Customer: Leave your card and I'll contact you if I need you.

You (Hesitate, smile, speak slowly as though there is something important which needs to be explained politely): I'll leave you my card with pleasure but *(hesitate just for a second for effect)* what I have to offer/say is very important and I don't think it would be helpful to you or to me if I just leave my card. I don't think you would be sorry if you gave me a few minutes to tell you how I can be of assistance to you/your business.

Customer: We can't shift the stock we've got from our existing people so we don't want more.

You (This is not a rebuff, it's an opening): A lot of my/our customers told me/us that before we supplied them. Our goods are _____ our prices are _____ /our packaging has a special appeal/our terms of credit/our display material/our advertising programme....

(When a potential customer cannot shift his old stock, you have a great opportunity. Tell him all about your product/service but do not knock your competitors. It is poor salesmanship and rarely produces a good effect. Your products and your service and, above all, you will speak for yourself.)

Customer: We are able to buy at the keenest prices in the business.

You (That answer is designed to put you right off. Don't let it): Do you only have one supplier?

Customer: We don't need more at their prices/We find them the most competitive/We've tried others in the past....

When existing suppliers fail

You (Speak confidently as though you are really worried about the client's business): Have you ever thought that it might be a safety-valve to have another supplier just in case you were ever let down? After all, if your present supplier ever failed to deliver, they'd also have to let other customers down. That might be a difficult time to try and establish goodwill with others.

(This approach was adopted by a salesman endeavouring to sell small hoses to a manufacturer of fire-fighting equipment. The latter had relied entirely on a German company for this product which was essential to its entire production. In the event, the manufacturer was persuaded to give 20 per cent of his business to the salesman. A year later, all the staff at the German company went on strike for a month. But for the salesman's initiative, the British manufacturer would have had a cash crisis as they would have been unable to obtain their equipment.)

Customer: You can't compete with the credit terms I get.

You (Do not consider this a rebuff but just another challenge. It should provide you with an opportunity to illustrate how your company works in the interest of its customers): What credit do you get?

(Or draw the customer out by telling him you give one month. If he is genuinely enjoying special credit terms, he is likely to tell you that he gets three months. This is the crunch point — repeat to yourself, 'Three months', and then turn to the customer. Remember that the three months is only two months more than you are offering him. That means that if the bank borrowing rate is 12 per cent per annum, the benefit for those extra two months amounts to only 2 per cent.)

A discount worth 250%

You: I must confess that we do not give three months' credit, but we offer you an immediate 5 per cent discount on all orders above £X *(make this figure worthwhile but not excessive).* Do you realise that that is 250 per cent more than getting three months' credit at the present time?

Customer: Sorry, I buy from an old friend of mine at my club/lodge/church/old scholars' association.

You (Difficult one to answer? Not if it's handled delicately. Consider roughly how much the customer might be spending a month — say £1,500. That means £18,000 a year. A 5 per cent discount would save him £900 — if you can afford 10 per cent, so much the better. Now the £18,000 turnover is probably producing a gross profit of around £6,000. Your 5 per cent discount represents 15 per cent of that profit): It's always nice if one can do business with old friends, but it can often be very expensive.

Learn your facts

The customer is bound to ask you to explain that statement. That is your opportunity. You might cite an example of a customer with a large turnover. This will make the real discount look so much higher. Being familiar with the calculation is very important, but even more so is having a clear idea in your mind of the maximum discount you can allow.

Every once in a while you have to take a chance when you feel that a really personal answer might rescue the situation. A good example is illustrated by an answer given by a young business man (Y.B.) from Leeds.

Customer: We don't change our suppliers, young man. We don't believe in it. We believe in loyalty.

The father touch

Y.B. (In a complimentary tone): You know, sir, you remind me of my father. He was a marvellous man and I respected him more than any man I ever met. Everybody liked him, but in the end his loyalty to old suppliers virtually ruined his business. *(He smiled thoughtfully and said half to himself)* I suppose that's why I had to start my own business.

This approach is a long shot but it has been proved to work. To be generously identified with the father of another person is a great compliment.

Whatever you decide to say to a potential customer to help you obtain an order, never, never plead that you need the order. Business men buy because they value the product or the service which they are being sold; they rarely wish to combine this with a charitable cause. Furthermore, remember that so long as you are in business, you must give the impression that you are in a good business in which you have every confidence. You are seeking orders not handouts.

The mirror to aid confidence

The vast majority of people experience enormous difficulty in introducing themselves to new customers, particularly when they have to face rebuffs. It is often worthwhile to follow the example of many outstanding speakers. They lock themselves in the room with the largest mirror and rehearse their speeches watching their facial expressions. Two men who built a large business from scratch used to visit every new customer together. Before doing so they rehearsed exactly what each one was going to say, trying to anticipate the questions that might be asked. They believed this was a major contribution to the success of their business. Anyone who has to sell for a living could find this exercise valuable. It justifies frequent practice.

DIY Businesses

This section includes examples of businesses which would be entirely dependent on your own efforts.

Unlike those listed under 'Agencies', the occupations covered by the next fifteen chapters do not require the co-operation of principals of other established businesses. Furthermore, in many cases the fundamentals are the same, as are the human qualities required to make the enterprises successful.

7

BOOK TRADING

No need to like books

A book-trader does not have to like books or even understand a great deal about them to be successful. It is a bonus if he does because he is likely to get pleasure as well as profit from the business.

Old books are different

The antiquarian and fine books market is highly specialised and is to be recommended only to those who have spent years with the specialists in this highly sophisticated world. One international expert, the late Heinrich Eisemann, once described how, as a young man, he spent several years with connoisseurs in Frankfurt, Paris, Rome and London before he ever actually purchased a book for sale. Eventually, this dignified gentleman was to figure among the great authorities in his field, his opinion regarded so highly that when he walked into the auction room at Sotheby's, respected buyers stood up. There are few Eisemanns in the world.

Trading for everyman

For the purpose of this chapter, consideration is only being given to trading in the type of second-hand books that fill the shelves of the average man. By and large, these range from collections of relatively unimportant first editions to volumes of poetry, books on cricket or business, autobiographies, novels and paperbacks. Often, there is the finely bound Bible inherited from an ancestor or a set of Dickens, Shakespeare or Sheridan. For the trader with no intellectual aspirations, he is concerned with buying books. Until he acquires any specialised knowledge, all he has to worry about is the selling prices.

Use initiative

Provided that he has a sound knowledge of the profit margins acceptable to bookshops, he can buy with confidence. This is not quite so simple as it sounds.

Know your selling prices

A second-hand bookseller in the West End of London may well sell a 1960 novel for £2, having paid no more than 30p for it. In a small village in Sussex or Durham, the local bookshop may well be selling the same book for £1, having also paid 30p for it.

The formula for success is to buy right. For that, one needs to carry out a reasonable amount of research, preferably in a major city as well as in provincial and suburban towns.

Trading with traders

With little experience and even less real knowledge, it is a lucky man who can make a steady profit from trading only with other traders. This might come with time and experience but it would be a fool who underestimates the pricing expertise of those who have spent their lives in the business.

Regardless of this, the opportunities for the newcomer to make money in the book business are numerous. The country auctions in the smaller towns frequently offer bargains because books are sold in lots. It is not uncommon for a miscellaneous collection of five hundred paperbacks to be knocked down for £25 or less.

600 per cent profit

This is a long way from the 30p a book which many established booksellers will pay; on this basis, the shrewd buyer could make a profit of over £100. This does not happen every day, but it does happen. The first art is to keep in touch with country and small town auctions. The second is to have a ready market to which you can sell. The latter is certainly not as difficult as the former.

Value goodwill highly

There are always buyers at the right price, and goodwill is established by building up a reputation with just a few booksellers whom you are able to supply regularly and who will pay promptly.

Attending auctions and looking for bargains is unlikely to give you the income you need, though, and certainly not if you are trading in the lower-priced books. Consequently, this form of trading can only be looked on as one side of your business.

Not just auctions

Even in the early stages, you could well cope with two other sides. The first is to familiarise yourself with the names of as many valuable books as possible. This category refers to special editions which booksellers are keen to acquire and for which they are prepared to pay well.

Know your market

Behind Bond Street is a bookseller who will pay high prices for first editions of the autobiographies and memoirs of many of the great politicians, if they are in good condition. Near Oxford is another trader who has a number of influential clients who are constantly pursuing him for eighteenth-century collections of Letters of The Famous. In Sussex resides an authority on Kipling who can never satisfy the demands he receives for first editions of Kipling's writings. A bookseller in Gateshead is constantly on the look-out for old books on Judaica. These are the areas where real money can be made, but it is essential that you know exactly what is required and the maximum that your prospective buyer will pay.

Be prepared to make mistakes and suffer disappointments, but perseverance will pay off. Every once in a while you will buy just one book for £20 and sell it for £200. At first, it will not happen very often, but knowledge, experience and, in particular, effort will influence its frequency.

But back to reality and the problem of making money from trading in everyday books. The question, surely, is Why wait for auctions? Once you have enough confidence to buy in the open market, you should be able to fix in your own mind exactly the price you will pay regardless of what other bidders are prepared to offer.

Use estate agents

The answer might be to contact estate agents for details of house-sales in order to advise vendors that you are a book buyer with funds available. This would seem a good idea but it is unlikely to work well in practice in all districts. In the 1980s, London agents, for instance, have been earning so much they could hardly devote any time to acting as intermediaries for buying and selling books. The average house-sale in a major city is likely to produce commissions of £1,000: on this basis their lack of interest is understandable, regardless of whether or not you are prepared to share your profits with them. The attitude in rural districts is often different, but there people are very conservative and it takes time to build goodwill and a worthwhile connection. That is something to bear in mind. In the meantime, you are concerned with early profits. The answer with the greatest odds in your favour is to make direct contact with owners of houses for sale.

Choosing your seller

Buying from unknown people is always difficult. You are not to know their age or their status. Many of them will not be remotely interested in selling their books, others will have bequeathed them to libraries or relatives. But there is likely to be a large minority who would genuinely welcome your enquiry. In order to maximise your chances, it would seem sensible to look for houses for sale in the more prosperous country villages. Here, people frequently wait to move until prompted by age or an inability to cope; and at such a time they tend to give away or sell their more valuable pieces of furniture and books. Anyone wishing to buy libraries can either write to estate agents advertising the properties or drive around looking for 'For Sale' signs. The latter method might be more productive in the long term as agents could get impatient with your enquiries.

A short letter to prospective sellers in the following vein could produce dividends. With a little investigation you should be able to discover their names. Address an individual wherever possible.

Polite short letter

Mrs K.L. Dawson
The Green Lodge,
Westhills, Cambs.

Dear Mrs Dawson,
If you are considering selling any of your books when you sell your home, I would welcome the opportunity of buying them.
Fortunately, I am able to offer the best prices and to arrange for books to be collected at any time to suit your convenience. Once an offer is made, it is entirely up to you whether or not you accept. It is the policy of my firm never to contact a client again unless requested to do so.
On this understanding, I do look forward to hearing from you.
Yours sincerely,

(Name)

Most people will not reply, which is just as well. If they did, you would not know how to handle the business. If you should be confronted with a fine selection of books, do not make any attempt to bid. Recognise the fact that you are out of your depth, but that you do not want to lose the deal altogether. Simply state that you believe that some of the books might be valuable and you would like a second opinion on them.

Take a partner

Immediately contact one of your up-market booksellers and, after negotiating a commission arrangement with him, introduce him to the prospective customer. This way, you will have a far better chance of completing the purchase. All sides will be happy, and you will also have enhanced the goodwill towards you of a knowledgeable bookseller. On the basis that he will expect to make an overall profit of around 100 per cent, you are fully entitled to seek an introduction commission of about 25 per cent.

Few fools in the book trade

It is important to emphasise that there are fewer fools in the second-hand book trade than in most others. They mostly know their trade and the profit margins which the market will stand. So long as people buy books, and millions do, there are always opportunities for new, honest traders to make a good living. It is not an alternative for someone who would be happier dealing in second-hand cars or temperamental horses.

Start with small lots

Without any basic knowledge, some experience is advisable. Failing that, only buy small lots in the early days. It may take you a little longer to make realistic profits, but you will be controlling the downside. Beginners can easily begin trading with a capital of £100-£200. Many a successful book-trader started his business buying in jumble sales.

8

CATERING ON A MINI-SCALE

People have been known to start up a coffee stall from the back of a converted caravan and to eke out a living from it. Others have launched sandwich bars in ideal locations only to discover that their overheads substantially exceeded their incomes.

Planning is a must

Catering is a world where few survive without careful planning, experience and adequate start-up capital. There are, of course, exceptions, particularly among the Asian community, where many are not only prepared to work harder than most but they also have enormous flair. In addition, their strong family bond often provides loyal, cheap labour during the crucial period when the business is being started. In general, inadequate capital and inexperience are formulas for disaster.

Money in sandwiches

There is, however, one profitable catering area which requires very little capital and carries almost no risk. It is the personal sandwich business, where one can accurately calculate overheads and profits on a daily basis. Factory, shop and office staff are ready customers for a variety of well-made, attractively packed, fresh sandwiches, and they are usually happy to pay more than café prices for the privilege of having their sandwiches brought to their doors, or even desks.

Quality not cheapness

The secrets of those who are successful are quality, courtesy and punctuality. A well-filled sandwich costs little more to make than a

46

mean one, but it can sell for a higher price. One is not obliged to be cheap in order to succeed. Offering made-to-order sandwiches is a treat which shops cannot provide because they are mostly too worried about their overheads. The worker who enjoys his ham-and-banana sandwich is not only perfectly prepared to pay for it, but loves to tell his friends all about it, too. Willingness to please at a personal level proves a great investment in this business. Finally, most of us are creatures of habit. When it comes to lunch-time, it is our stomachs sooner than our watches which tell us that we are ready for a meal.

Punctuality is essential

Deliveries on time, without the customer having to leave the premises or queue, gives the private sandwich-maker an edge on his commercial competitor.

Start with £30

To get started, you only need about £30 to buy from a cash-and-carry store sufficient ingredients to last for two days. Of course, goods like salt, pepper and ketchup will probably last longer. A look round a sandwich bar will give you a very clear idea of selection, and enable you to make a rough estimate of which sandwiches are more popular than others.

Keep them fresh

Planning the making of the sandwiches is important. Good, well-filled sandwiches take time to make and pack. Furthermore, they have to be ready in time for you to reach your first customer no later than midday. It makes good sense therefore to prepare most if not all your fillings the night before. Sliced bread can be buttered and kept in a fridge overnight, and grated cheese and eggs are none the worse for being kept in a cool, covered dish.

With your open basket to display your wares, you follow the tracks to small local factories and other business establishments.

Small firms pay well

There is usually little point in calling on the larger factories as they invariably have their own canteens providing subsidised lunches. Wherever you are well received it is good to let the management know that you also provide sandwiches for working lunches.

Expansion ideas

These can be particularly profitable as an element of one-upmanship comes into it, which is reflected in orders for smoked salmon and other more expensive fillings.

Cash and carry

Of course, the profit margin in such cases is much higher as the average cash-and-carry prices for good smoked salmon can be less than half that of the slightly better-quality smoked salmon sold in most superior food stores. With a little sprinkling of lemon, there are few who can tell the difference.

Know your customers

Keen football fans make very good customers, especially if you are prepared to deliver their fresh sandwiches with a packet of crisps and possibly a bar of chocolate just before they leave work for mid-week matches. Small plastic bags are very useful to prevent leaking, but double-packing can be an effective alternative. Everyone will appreciate that the profit margin for this service is higher.

Sandwiches almost sell themselves, but not quite. They do need to be presented in an appetising way.

Dress clean, look clean

Equally important, the vendor, namely yourself, should always appear clean, tidy and (if you're a man) well-shaved. It does not matter how unkempt some of your customers may be, most sober people like their food prepared and served by those who look washed and have clean fingernails.

Sandwich prices do vary in different parts of the country and even between areas in the same city. In parts of London and Manchester, for example, it is possible to buy large pieces of bread with poor fillings for 60p, but good-value-for-money sandwiches cost up to £1.00 or £1.90 for a filling such as salmon.

Profits run at 200 per cent

The independent vendor can afford to keep his prices near the top end, and the profit margin, so long as you are making the sandwiches yourself and using your own kitchen, is in the region of 200 per cent.

To expand or not

There could easily come a time when you have to decide whether to expand or not. Without expansion a steady profit can be made every week, giving you plenty of time for study, sport or any other hobby. You can usually reckon to finish before 2 p.m. most days.

What expansion means

Expansion, of course, means more customers, more overheads, higher profits and less free time. These must all be acceptable if you are keen to build a real business from your modest beginnings, and your confidence that this is the right step to take will no doubt be fired by your recognising greater scope for sales. This only leaves you with the problem of finding the right help.

The simplest way to recruit assistants is to place advertisements in local shop windows. The chances are that your kitchen is not suitable for more than one pair of hands, so, while a satisfactory applicant should be able to produce a sandwich to your high standards, even more important, he or she should keep a spotless kitchen. Terms of employment, however informal, must include kitchen inspection.

Watch the hazards

Apart from any health hazards, you simply cannot afford to risk prejudicing goodwill by offering sandwiches that may carry hairs or generally appear unwholesome. Always pay piece-work rather than hourly rates; 17p a sandwich is considered a fair rate when all the ingredients are delivered to, and the sandwiches collected from, the outworker's home. The total cost of producing the average sandwich, in relatively small quantities, in 1991, is around 40p. Obviously, smoked salmon sandwiches, for instance, would be more expensive. The gross profit margin, depending on the quality of the sandwich, varies between 40 and 100 per cent. In the Midlands, the North of England and poorer districts, the profit margins are lower.

Large profits are possible

Mini-catering can be consistently profitable, with great scope and little downside. Two sisters who started such a business in London, purely for pin money, found themselves selling nearly 1,000 sandwiches a day within three years. In 1986, that gave them a six-figure annual profit. They then began catering for parties and weddings, an expansion programme which necessitated recruiting a third partner with the required experience. This presented little problem, and their second successful business is now registered as a separate company. The reason for this is twofold. The first is to give the new partner a share in the business in which she works, and the second is to facilitate its sale, if necessary, without disposing of the sandwich business, or vice-versa.

Important

Know the laws of hygiene

Before you start any business directly or even indirectly connected with supplying food to the public, you should read Food Hygiene Regulations 1970, and the Food Hygiene (Amendments) Regulations 1990 which directly affects sandwich-makers. There are numerous regulations under the Food Act 1984 and the Food Safety Act 1990 which relate to the handling of food, the premises on which it is prepared, the disposal of waste and relevant matters which affect hygiene. It is not at all uncommon for people to blame some form of food poisoning or lesser stomach ailment on any food which was not prepared at their own home. Even successfully defending such an accusation can prove prohibitively expensive — so you would be well advised to effect appropriate third-party insurance to cover you against any real or imaginary claim for food poisoning.

9

FLOWER MAKING

The subject of this chapter falls into a special category. Unlike any of the others, it depends largely on two additional factors.

Loving flowers helps

The first is that people who love flowers are likely to be the best at making artificial ones. The second is that without any previous experience one is obliged to start the business as just a hobby.

There is considerable potential for those who can master the art of making beautiful flowers, and the great attraction is that it requires very little money to get started.

You can start with £25

There are indeed very few worthwhile businesses that can be started on the kitchen table with a capital of about £25. But it must be recognised by anyone wishing to start in this field that they are hoping to make a business from an art. It is one that requires considerable patience and perseverance and, like all other artistic endeavours, can cause enormous frustration to beginners.

Materials available

Most of the equipment required to start a flower-making business can be purchased from florists, DIY and hardware stores, chemists and handicrafts shops. There are, of course, classes that can be attended and they probably offer the best way of getting trained. *Floodlight,* the yearly publication that lists hundreds of adult-education classes held in the London area, might well prove a useful buy. However, the more confident and artistically inclined could well achieve success from following the instructions given in a good book

Good books to read

There are quite a number of these, but two quite helpful ones are *Making Silk Flowers* by Anne Hamilton and Kathleen White, published by Merehurst, and *Paper Flower Sculpture* by Jeanne Westcott, published by Blandford Press.

If this growing artistic business appeals to you, the marketing advice given in other chapters in this book may easily be applied. Once you begin to get regular orders, you might consider starting a small training class. From this, it should not be difficult to establish your own cottage industry.

Hints to note

Words of advice:
1. Quality sells more than price.
2. Do not carry a large stock.
3. Apart from flower-lovers, there is a big market in supplying hotels, boutiques, shops and offices, doctors' and dentists' waiting-rooms.
4. If in doubt, start it off as a hobby and develop it as a sideline first.
5. Shoddy workmanship will not sell, but there are increasing numbers of people paying high prices for quality.

10

FRAMING

The art of making attractive frames can become a great hobby which, in turn, could lead to an enjoyable small business. However, competing with mass production of cheap frames would present many difficulties as one would be dealing with a very modestly priced article with little room for useful profit margins.

It must make more than pocket-money

It could certainly be a 'pocket-money' exercise for anyone seeking a modest profit to augment an existing income. An interesting thought, but this book is not about pocket-money ventures. It is about starting businesses, with very modest capital, which have every chance of success within a reasonable time. Framing does not fall into that category.

Think it through

To dismiss the entire subject at this stage would be to ignore the real possibility of building a highly profitable business from a framing-related idea. An enterprise that could offer great opportunities for imagination and job satisfaction. The recommended thinking process is to consider the end product: who buys frames? What do they frame? Why?

The pretty frame is largely purchased for family photographs — weddings, children and grandparents, or when someone is honoured or decorated. Other standard types of old and modern frames are used by picture galleries and those people who hang paintings and drawings in their homes. There has been an enormous increase in the sales of posters in recent years but these tend to be pinned unframed to walls.

Encourage interest

In practice, very few people in England spend much money on books and even less on art. There is certainly scope for encouraging far greater interest, but that is probably a reflection on our education system rather than on our artists or our art galleries. Sadly, the English are not really into culture in a very big way. They love their gardens, their pets and their pubs, and are happy to admire the work of their favourite artists in the museums. A poorly written paperback thriller might sell 100,000 copies but a first-class novel will be lucky to sell over 10,000, and it's generally much less.

Markets can be too small

In the average home, there are usually fewer than six prints or any works of art that have required framing. Although there are no accurate figures, it is estimated that less than 15 per cent of the population have drawings, paintings, sketches or prints adorning their walls. In the private sector, it is for this small minority that too many frame-makers offer a service. But there is still a large, almost untapped, market for the imaginative entrepreneur in the framing business. The answer is to stop thinking of frames and, instead, concentrate your mind on words like images, decorations, interest, amusement, vanity, and prestige.

Look at the wallpaper

There are many thousands of offices and showrooms that look better or more finished because someone has put a few pictures on the walls. The exciting fact is that there are many thousands more with bare walls, and even greater numbers of others whose occupants persist in re-hanging the same ageing prints each time the wallpaper is changed. These are the areas where opportunities for making money are waiting for anyone with imagination and initiative. There is little to be gained from wandering round busy firms of solicitors, accountants and advertising agents trying to sell frames. The answer is to move a step further and question what each practitioner is likely to find decorative which is already framed.

It is not just the frames

The prints of famous cartoonists like Spy, Bateman, Heath Robinson and Low can often be purchased for relatively little, as can prints of old colleges, cities or ancestral homes by men like Shepherd. They are not difficult to find in large numbers, just waiting to be bought for nominal amounts. A broad plan of campaign might well be the following:

Finding the answers

1. Visit a good variety of junk shops, local art exhibitions and bookshops, and take your time examining hundreds of different prints, drawings and water-colours. It is still possible to pick up old editions of beautifully

FRAMING

illustrated books on buildings, birds, gardens, soldiers, horses, cars, battles, well-known characters, and numerous other subjects. Such books can be among your best buys as they invariably offer the cheapest way of acquiring delightful subjects for framing.

Use your imagination

2. Try to imagine how a small collection would look together on a wall. Possibly a group of seventeenth- and eighteenth-century soldiers, individual drawings of twentieth-century judges, or coloured prints of famous houses, universities, theatrical costumes, flowers or ships. The combinations are endless. But allow yourself time, and invest in a few of the better home magazines. They are full of ideas and photos. If you cannot quite picture such collections, call in on a few of the better interior decorators or visit museums, libraries and art galleries. Make a note of any fine, suitable books you see in libraries. Then take your list to a good second-hand bookshop and ask them to try and locate copies.

Use a good free service

Antiquarian booksellers have their own publication specifically for this purpose. They make no charge for the enquiry, advertising, or for actually finding the book you want. It is an excellent service, particularly as you can always decline to buy if you consider the prices too high. You are about to start a profitable business, so do not expect to become an instant expert. Few of us are born with flair in this field but fortunately it can be acquired.

3. Shop around to find a good framer who also understands the importance of choosing the mounts carefully. Although it is the picture that first appeals to the customer, it is often the mount and the frame that persuade him to buy it. A well-established framer is usually able to offer sound advice on what goes with what on a wall, and while this, of course, varies with individual taste, such professional guidance is invaluable. You are not just buying his frames, you are getting years of expertise and experience thrown in at no extra cost.

Testing the market

4. Having had one or two sets of six water-colours or prints framed, you are ready to test the market. You are about to present a firm with the opportunity to add colour, interest and a little style to their office walls. If a set has cost you, say, £90, you will aim to sell it for £180. This gives you a reasonable profit, bearing in mind the time you spent finding the prints, calling on the framer and visiting your customer. You are selling a concept, not a substitute for wallpaper.

However you dress, you should endeavour to give the impression that you are someone with good taste and not someone who finds their clothes on tips.

A gentle sales approach

5. If you are nervous about making your first call, you could try an approach that might give you greater confidence. You can ask your bank manager for an introduction to a firm of solicitors, or you could simply look up the name

of a firm in a directory. Either way, telephone and endeavour to be put through to the senior partner. If he is busy, give your name boldly to the telephonist, try to ascertain when he will be free and promise to phone back. Eventually you will get through, and you will have rehearsed exactly what you are going to say.

Do not rush

At this stage, you are not selling anything, you are carrying out a little market research. You might start this way:

The first call

'Good afternoon, Mr Burrell, my name is Christopher Simpkins, and I am collating the opinions of leading professionals in this town.'
Whoever he is, the little man inside him will be flattered. You are seeking his opinion and you have rated him a leading professional. He is listening to you, so don't lose the advantage.
  Continue:
'The idea is to invite a limited number of lawyers to give their opinions on suitable art forms for professional offices. It would be extremely helpful to have your views.'
'Who are you exactly, Mr Simpkins?' is the question for which you must have a ready answer, albeit that you give it slowly.
'I am a member of a small group concerned with establishing the extent to which discerning professionals consider that art enhances the appearance of their offices.' Then add casually, 'It's really to obtain the opinions of a number of people of good taste.'
Mr Burrell will more than likely grant you an interview. If you discover that he already has well-covered walls, it could be to your distinct advantage. First, if you like them, admire them; you can immediately comment on how few members of the profession take so much trouble or have such a discerning eye. Secondly, if Mr Burrell's pictures are yellowed and dusty, you can ask him if he has ever thought of changing them.

The questionnaire

6. When you unwrap your collection, also produce a pad on which to make notes of his reactions to your questions:
* Does he like them?
* Would clients find them interesting?
* Would he prefer them in the waiting-room or in his office?
* Do any of his partners have pictures on their walls?
* Does he think that solicitors would like to have art on their walls in preference to or in addition to their various certificates?
* Would they find it more interesting if the selection could be changed from time to time?

Notes not only impress

The notes you are making are not just to impress Mr Burrell. They are to give you something solid to discuss with your next potential customer. You will be able to quote the (helpful) opinions of a senior partner of a highly respected firm without, of course, mentioning his name. Do not bring up the subject of money. Mr Burrell will do that regardless of whether or not he buys. If he buys, fine. If not, you should have a very good idea why not. After ten such meetings, read all your notes and make fresh ones of the lessons you have learned so far. You might consider establishing your business as *Art Advisers to Professional Offices*. Remember to use good-quality stationery.

Once you are confident that you are the right person in the right business, a number of major decisions need to be made.

Who makes the frames?

1. Should you consider having your frames specially made? If the saving is nominal you will do far better to negotiate special prices with two or three good framers and support them. Your business is to concentrate on new and existing customers.

Another profitable option

2. Check out whether any of your professional friends would find it more interesting to hire the selection, rather than buy it. The attraction of this alternative could be your willingness to change the selection three times a year. For this you would make a small charge. You might consider it reasonable to suggest a three-year agreement at £X a month, but you should check out whether someone like Mr Burrell would consider your prices reasonable or extortionate. The right rental figure must give you a good return on your sale price, which means an excellent profit on your cost price: e.g., if you are offering a set of framed prints for £200, it should be quite acceptable for you to charge 12 per cent including your selection-change service.

Your bank will love this business

This would give you a return of 24 per cent per annum on your costs and a reason to re-visit Mr Burrell, hopefully for introductions. This is the type of business which your bank, or any other bank, would love to help you develop.

Now think of advertising

3. When the business begins to tick, it will be because you have thought through and worked through every stage yourself. This will be the time to consider a 'Livewire' advertisement. The successful applicant should only be concerned with servicing existing customers and finding new ones. You will not make him familiar with your buying secrets, your framing costs or how you cope with them. Your Livewire has just one function — to help you build your enterprise, not to become a competitor.

4. If the above figures make sense, you will only need three or four customers a week who buy or rent to earn a good living. More than that and you can be grateful to whoever made you redundant.

11

A FURNITURE BUSINESS

How John and Brian started

For a number of years John X had been a highly competent foreman in a modern furniture factory. Previously, he had trained to be a carpenter and joiner, and had studied furniture design at evening classes. One day a colleague, Brian Y, pointed out that the cheap end of the office-furniture market was virtually neglected. Firmly believing that an opportunity to make a fortune was staring at them, they decided to pack up their jobs and launch themselves into this new, highly specialised, business. With the assistance of an enterprising accountant and an agreeable investment banker, the two men raised half a million pounds through a business expansion scheme. Their credentials spoke for them, and a number of high tax payers were quickly persuaded that it would be good business to provide the capital. Ideal premises were found, staff were quickly recruited, stock and machines purchased and detailed estimates made. The local newspaper congratulated the directors on their initiative, and the factory was opened by the deputy mayor of the town. A year later, with capital spent and debts accumulating, the company went into liquidation.

A sad story

It was a sad story which has been often repeated in recent years. John and Brian, both honest men, had committed the following common errors.

The errors they made

First Error: Having worked on the production side of a large company, they believed they understood every aspect of the business.

Second Error: They confused the ability to play a significant role in a well-established team in an existing business with the qualifications required to start a new one.

Third Error: They failed to realise or ascertain the reasons why other manufacturers avoided the cheap end of the office furniture market. The reasons were that:

* Even small businesses are not keen on buying cheap furniture if they can possibly help it.
* If there was a profitable market, a relatively small business like their own would find it extremely difficult to face the existing competition or the competition they would generate.
* The cheaper end of most markets requires the longest credit terms and produces the largest number of debts.

But do not be put off

This true story, though typical of many, should not deter anyone from starting in the furniture business in a modest way. The following approach, which applies to launching any small manufacturing business, can create the maximum dividends with the minimum risk. The rules are simple but important. The potential downside is very small and so is the initial financial commitment.

The right way to start

The basic rules of starting a low-risk manufacturing business are as follows:

1. Carefully consider the maximum amount of capital you can afford to *lose*. For this purpose, all loans and bank borrowings should be ignored. Then decide that this is your working capital until the business begins to tick over.
2. Consider the income you believe you need to enjoy the standard of living which you would like to achieve. Then double it. The additional amount represents your challenge and your real profit.
3. Make up your mind to pay all bills promptly.
4. Avoid any customers who require credit.
5. Initially, only consider a business that you can operate from home. If the ideal place is your garage, check that your car is fully insured if it is to be left outside all night. Also check whether you require extra insurance protection for goods stored in your garage, and third-party insurance.

Think about easy production

6. Choose an object the production of which can easily be sub-contracted to retired craftsmen or handymen and women.

7. Aim at a business which will bring you into direct competition with manufacturers you would expect to have large overheads — e.g. modern premises, expensive machinery, well-paid staff, spacious offices. Consider all the reasons why it should be possible to operate a similar business on a smaller scale.

Write out your plan

8. Write out and re-write exactly how you see your operation working. Build a programme which precisely covers the timing and financing of your purchases, your out-workers, collections, deliveries and payments on account. The accent should always be on economy of both time and expenditure, but not of quality. The following is an illustration:

A real example

A very simple television table costs a retailer £60, and he sells it for £75-80. This enables him to reduce the price to a maximum of £65 in a sale and still make a small profit. On this basis, it is reasonable to assume that to be competitive a new manufacturer should aim to produce a table to sell for £50 allowing for a net profit of at least £10. This is *after* allowing for the cost of rent (if any), materials, labour, production, stationery, telephones, postage, delivery charges and advertising. This is a real possibility bearing in mind that he would be working from his garage, with no paid staff, no employment stamps, no sickness and holiday pay, little additional heating or electricity, no rent, no depreciation of expensive machinery and no advertising. If the sums look like the following, then you are in business.

Costing in detail

Per table	
Raw materials and labour	£30.00
Delivery charges and telephones	.65
Postage and petrol	1.00
Margin for error	3.35
Profit	15 .00
Selling price	£50.00

On this basis there is a more than adequate margin for higher costs of labour and materials, as well as for possible discounts on larger orders.

The first steps to production

The first steps to take are:

1. Buy a TV table and carefully take it to pieces.
2. Consider any adaptations. It may be possible slightly to improve the design to make it serve equally well as a coffee table.
3. Draw plans for each piece of wood. You do not need to be a draughtsman; simply note down the measurements of the length, breadth and width. This is all the local timber yard will require in order to cut the wood exactly to size. Order enough to make three tables.
4. Without rushing, sandpaper the pieces to a fine finish, assemble them and paint them with a coat of varnish. Make a note of the time taken. Repeat this twice more, each time making a note of how long it took. This will give you a reasonable idea of the average time required to make a table ready for sale.
5. Show the table to at least three local furniture dealers to establish whether they would be prepared to pay £50 for it. If it appears doubtful, remember that you have a fair margin to negotiate.

How to find staff

6. Only at this point, when you are confident that you can produce a good product at a saleable price, do you take the next step. Advertise in a *local* newspaper for retired handymen interested in working at home. Expect to be inundated with replies.
7. Visit a number of applicants nearest to your home as they are going to be the most conveniently placed for you to work with. If they do not have a sample of their own handiwork to show you, offer to give them pieces of a table to assemble. That is the time you can tell them the price you are prepared to pay them for assembling each table.

Do not pay time-rates

Always pay a piece-rate rather than a time-rate.
8. On the basis that each table will produce a net profit of £15, you will need to build up production and sell about twenty-five a week to make a pre-tax profit of marginally under £20,000 per annum. At this stage you have to decide whether to market your tables over a larger area or to start making an additional small item.
9. Once you are satisfied that you can rely on sufficient production to yield a given profit, you must become an enthusiastic salesman.

Now for sales

Begin by covering the area within a radius of five miles from your home. Always ensure that you make it clear that you can only offer your prices on the basis of cash on delivery. Beware of the large firms who try to buy your entire production. They play on the greed buttons of their suppliers and have ruined far more small business men than they have made. Small businesses should never be dependent for more than 20 per cent of their business on any one customer.

Advice time

10. This is the point when you would do well to visit a local chartered accountant. He should be happy to advise you on all aspects of tax, including VAT, and every expense which can legally be claimed against your profits. If a small company is to be formed, it could be an excellent idea to put up to half the shares in the names of your spouse and/or children. It will not affect the salary that you draw, but it could be very useful if you ever decide to sell any of the shares. Some might argue that such action is looking a long way ahead but that is what tax planning is all about. The accountant should be competent to advise you on this and any other financial aspect of the business.

Use more than one supplier

11. Orders for separate table parts should be placed with different timber yards. In this way, you are not dependent on one supplier. Furthermore, it reduces the chances of creating competition. You should find that timber yards are prepared to give you two weeks' credit, which should be more than adequate.

Other examples

There is no doubt that this operation can be applied equally successfully to numerous products which are normally manufactured in expensive factories with high overheads. Good examples are garden furniture, casual clothing, picture frames, light fittings, leather goods and items for the car and the home. With the large number of capable unemployed, and those who have taken early retirement, there is no shortage of labour for cottage industries.

Follow the golden rules

The following golden rules are always worth observing:
* AVOID producing cheap items with only nominal profit margins.
* AVOID specialist suppliers of raw materials who might let you down — e.g. importers and foreign manufacturers.
* AVOID articles which require considerable expertise in their production.
* AVOID customers who insist on credit. Offer a discount if necessary but do remember that you are not in competition with the banks. After all, if the customer cannot obtain additional credit from his bank, why should you provide it?
* AVOID demands which could impose pressure on your bank balance, your family or your lifestyle.

SPECIAL NOTES

Places for ideas

The best places to look for ideas are large department stores, chemists, furniture shops, car suppliers and the mail-order pages of the more upmarket magazines.

Finally, and of great importance: keep your business secrets to yourself. Remember, your aim is to create profits, not competition.

12

GIFTS

Profits and competition

Every single day of every year, in good and bad times, countless thousands of expensive and inexpensive, personal and impersonal, presents are given. Despite the size of this emotional and commercial market, one needs to tread carefully before attempting to get into it. Not only are there numerous suppliers in this country already but foreign manufacturers have been successfully creating competition for many years. Perhaps more significant, foreign labour costs are often very low and their profit margins frequently unrealistically high. It is not uncommon for an item to be purchased for under £1 in Hong Kong and sold for £5 in London. The trouble is that in England we often cannot even produce the same article for £5.

All is not entirely lost, but it does make it much more important to carry out one's research very carefully.

Pricing right

Well-finished goods hand-crafted to a high standard can usually find a market, albeit at a price. Still, it is better to sell five hundred articles, with limited competition, for £20 each than two thousand at £5 with all the manufacturers in Taiwan waiting to copy it.

Initially, a great deal can be learned by wandering around major stores and top-class gift shops. In each case, the two important details to notice are where an item was produced, and what it sells for. At this stage you could save considerable time by deleting all items from your list that are made in the Far East.

Check Swiss goods

Equally, note articles produced in Switzerland — costs there are often very high, thereby making it possible to compete in the UK.

Avoid capital investments

You should further reduce your list by all items that are virtually impossible to manufacture without a major capital investment. Lastly, do not include very expensive products. Even if you believe you could produce them more cheaply, it is unlikely that you would find enough competent out-workers to enable you to build a business.

What can be made

You might therefore come down to items like spectacle cases, aprons, finely made slippers, bolster cushions, paperweights, table mats and similar items. Even the smallest lending library has a good selection of DIY books with detailed instructions on how to make all these and many more items. If you have a good eye for colour and design, you could for instance make a useful profit from producing attractive cushions. The reason for picking on cushions rather than one of the many other possible items is that the prices vary more. A really beautiful cushion might well sell to the public for £20-£30. This would mean that the supplier would be ready to pay no more than £12-£18. To compete in that market, allowing yourself a fair profit, you may have to make it for no more than £5-£10. Labour might be readily available, particularly in rural areas where many women still practise skills relevant to the craft, but the problem would be finding quality silks with fine designs. The best purchases are likely to be made from ends-of-lines and you would need to wander round almost constantly looking for suitable pieces.

Is it a hobby or a business?

On balance, gift-making might best be left to those who are seeking a profitable hobby rather than a business with potential. This is not a defeatist attitude; it is simply an acknowledgement that other chapters in this book probably illustrate easier ways for you to make a good living. The one exception is toys and this is dealt with as a separate subject on pages 98-103.

However, there are some useful books which could give you some ideas. These include *Cushions and Covers* by Sue Locke, published by Ward Lock, and *45 Great Gifts to Make* by Jean Greenhowe, published by David & Charles. The latter contains ideas for gifts such as patchwork quilts, gift baskets and pin cushions.

13

GLASS ENGRAVING

An artistic business

This chapter is included specifically for readers who would like to be involved in an artistic business. Those who can already draw will find themselves at a distinct advantage, but almost anyone with patience, a steady hand, and some powers of concentration can produce delightful glass engravings. It is still a good idea to acquire some drawing skill.

A book to read and enjoy

It would also be helpful to read a few books on the subject. These can readily be found in any good local library. *The Art and Technique of Glass Engraving* by Majella Taylor and Noreen Cooke is full of useful information for the beginner. Other useful books to read are *Glass Engraving, Lettering and Design* by David Peace, published by Batsford, and *Glass Engraving* by Jonathan Matcham and Peter Dreiser, also published by Batsford.

Courses in glass engraving can be taken at most evening classes. It is important to remember that a little experience will not make you a great artist but it should enable you to start a profitable small business in an area where there is still considerable scope.

Where to start

A set of hand tools is not expensive, and it would probably be wise to commence learning with them. However, there are a number of economical electric drills available and obviously you will need one of these if you hope to produce work commercially. There are quite a number of companies supplying this equipment and it would be worthwhile contacting them before making any purchases.

Where to buy

One such company is Charles Cooper (Hatton Garden) Ltd, 23-27 Hatton Wall, London EC1N 8JJ.

Marketing for selling

The initial problem for most glass engravers is marketing. The easiest outlets to find are stores and gift shops but, of course, you have to sell goods to them at no more than two-thirds of the retail selling price. This means that your own profit must be nominal if you are to be competitive. The alternative is to find private customers.

Types of customer

This might seem a rather difficult task on an on-going basis, but need not be so. A practical approach would be to place your potential customers into three classes: private, social and commercial.

The private customer is likely to be interested in two or three types of glass engraving. First, a name; second, an animal; and lastly a property. There are countless people who would love to have their own home or pet engraved on a glass. You may well find that a local shop would be happy to have a selection of your work in their windows. If so, they would be equally pleased to collect orders for a reasonable commission of, say, 10 per cent. You could also advertise in shop windows for part-time agents — something along the following lines:

A useful advertisement

PART-TIME AGENTS WANTED
Lucrative opportunity for part-time agents. No fixed hours.
No stock. No capital outlay. No experience or training necessary.
A good social circle could prove very useful.
Phone: _____

Social sales outlets

The social category would include bridge clubs, golf clubs, tennis clubs, schools, ladies' guilds, etc., many of which would be delighted to sell glasses with their own name and crest. It takes no time at all to engrave a pair of golf clubs above a scroll with the name of a golf club. If ten clubs only sold one glass a week each, it would be good business particularly as you would not have to give any commission away.

Commercial outlets

The commercial category would be hotels. Americans and other guests love to collect souvenirs and they don't all stick to ashtrays. One engraver in a seaside resort reckons to produce at least twenty glasses a week during the summer season. Furthermore, the business card which he inserts in each glass produces a steady flow of orders all the year round.

Showing up your work

Constant practice improves style, and the finer the work, the more one can charge. A useful little trick of the trade is to brush talcum powder over the engraving and then gently wipe it off. It shows the artwork up beautifully.

Careful packing

Finally, visit a shop that sells packing materials. These can be extremely useful, if not essential, in delivering or posting orders. You may find that the local china store would be happy for you to take away some of the materials in which deliveries to them have been packed.

14

GRAVE CARE

A STEADY BUSINESS

Very sad facts

An inspection of any cemetery will show a large number of neglected graves. This sad situation arises more from lack of thought than from real indifference. There are always exceptions, but the average person does not bury a parent or relation with a decision to allow their grave to become overgrown — most have a marked respect for the memories of loved ones whom they have lost. Statistics show that second only to talking about their children and grandchildren, people enjoy recalling the pleasures shared with departed parents.

Services available

Many of the larger cemeteries do provide a maintenance service, but only about a third of the families of the departed seem to use it. It would appear that this often comes about because people initially plan to take care of the graves themselves, and when they cease to do so, they feel too embarrassed to ask the cemetery superintendent to make the appropriate arrangements. In the case of the smaller cemeteries, such a service is often not available.

Customer sources

Here, surely, is an opportunity for enterprising people to provide a service business which must always be in demand. The best sources for customers are Church ministers and undertakers. The former should be only too pleased to mention your services on their notice-board or in the parish magazine. It would be a comfort to thousands of old and not so old people to know that they might be relieved of such responsibilities, for with the best will in the world, there comes a time when age or bad weather prevents people from visiting graves regularly. Undertakers, of course, have years of records of those whom they have buried. They may well be inclined to offer the service on your behalf.

Publicity can be cheap and effective

Once you have decided to go into this business, it would be a good idea to let the local newspapers know about it: there's a chance that they would feature your business in a prominent position. But, good business though it may be, it would be quite easy to get it wrong. To avoid this, the following steps are suggested:

Research is important

1. Carry out your own research. Visit all the cemeteries in your area and:
* Make notes of the approximate percentage of neglected graves.
* Make notes of the percentage of such graves applicable to people buried in the last fifteen years — relatives who have neglected graves for longer are either not interested or unlikely to be easily traceable.
* Check with the resident superintendent that there would be no objection to your providing the service.
2. Find out if any similar services exist in the area. If they do, it is possible that there might not be room for competition. In any event, find out what their charges are.
3. Do not attempt to follow up potential customers concerned with graves in small cemeteries unless you believe there are likely to be enough to make your effort worthwhile. Remember, you are running a business, not a charity.

Avoid one-off jobs

4. Do not undertake one-off jobs. They will never pay. You must be retained for at least a year, and calculate your charges according to the number of visits the customer would like you to make.
5. Tidying graves, and possibly planting a few flowers or bushes, is not a difficult task. Cleaning tombstones, however, requires more expertise. This work is often undertaken by specialist firms. You might be able to obtain an agency from one or two in return for notifying them of interested customers.

Add a photo service

6. Many customers would love to know how you are looking after the graves. It could be an investment to buy a small Polaroid camera and let them see photographs of the graves before and after you have cared for them. This is the type of extra service that people will talk about.
7. Do remember that potential customers might well be in a state of grief when you approach them — and do bear it in mind that other potential customers would not appreciate any implication that they are showing disrespect to their dead by neglecting their graves — so, be sympathetic and tactful.

71

Expansion possibilities

This business has some potential, but it is unlikely to grow rapidly. Ideally, anyone going into it should aim to provide the service for the maximum number of graves in as few cemeteries as possible. Window cards and small advertisements can be helpful, but remember that customers are unlikely to pay you more than about £30-35 a year. As many people like flowers to be laid on anniversaries and birthdays, you might check whether there is scope for a joint business with local florists. They could, for instance, easily offer a 'Grave Care Service' on your behalf.

As this is a time-consuming business, the only way you can possibly expand is to encourage others to join you on a fee-sharing basis. You would probably have to limit your own share to about 10 per cent.

Once this business is established, you are unlikely ever to be unemployed again, but you must not expect to make a fortune out of it.

15

JUNK TRADING

Think of useful junk

Most readers will associate the title of this chapter with the little man with a raucous voice who travels round the back streets of small towns collecting old baths, bent cycle wheels, broken tiles, gates, gas-stoves, and other refuse that clutters up garages, gardens and back yards. Somehow, those characters have managed to earn their keep throughout the ages. This chapter is not about their stock in trade. It is about useful junk, or junk that could be made useful.

You can become a junk lover

It is a business for the natural potterer, the dreamer with imagination, the lover of pretty objects — those who want to enjoy whatever it is that is going to provide them with a living. Such people know that selling insurance or other intangible services might well make them lots of money, but they are happy to make less and derive real pleasure in doing so from being an observant wanderer.

Where to find stock

Junk-buying and -selling is not the shallow end of the antique business. It is trading in a wide variety of interesting, unusual or pretty articles that have been discarded because their owners failed to recognise their use or their value. They are objects to be found in second-hand shops, jumble sales and on market stalls. They range from broken clocks and instruments to small pieces of furniture, china, silver, plate, toby jugs and old toys, and hundreds of odd things that different people loved in days gone by.

Imagination is a great asset

The successful junk-trader needs to know who will buy what and how much it is worth; then he knows what he is looking for. As he learns the business, he will recognise items which can readily be used for purposes for which they were never designed. One lady dealer, walking round an untidy little shop in Newcastle, spotted a hundred small Victorian buckles. An apparently useless package for £5. She bought them, and in less than an hour had cleaned them all up with a little silver polish. She then joined pairs together with pretty pieces of ribbon and sold forty bookmarks to an up-market gift shop for £400. She kept the remainder for her own stock. Another trader, looking for unusual clocks, stumbled across half a dozen old photographs in a South London backstreet. The photos were of no interest but the dirty frames were delightfully designed. He bought them for £1 each, and after cleaning them up sold them for twenty times that figure to a shop in Bond Street.

Frames and old kettles are good business

A middle-aged couple were about to give up the idea of trading in junk when the wife spotted a very discoloured nineteenth-century kettle with a bent spout. She bought it for £2. As she cleaned away the layers of dirt she discovered it was made of copper. She filled it up with artificial flowers and sold it for £100 to an antique dealer. Today, that couple make an excellent living trading almost exclusively in 'junk' suitable for flower arrangements. In Yorkshire lives a man who for many years has made a steady income from small colourful pieces of old silk and carpets. He cuts them up, frames the pieces, and sells them to interior decorators. It is not quite as easy as it sounds, however, as all these people may have travelled for days, if not weeks, without finding anything worth buying, or before deciding to specialise.

An ideal fun business

Junk-buying is a fun business. It is ideal for men and women with shrewd eyes and creative minds — realistic, observant people who do not expect to be sold a bargain but rather believe that they can create one. There is no money in rubbish, junk on the other hand offers real opportunities.

It might be said that there are many traders who buy junk but sell antiques!

16

MATCHING

THE IDEAL BUSINESS FOR THE TRADER AND ABSOLUTELY PERFECT FOR THE ENTREPRENEUR

There is probably no business with more possibilities than that of matching — a form of broking, operating on the same principle as a marriage bureau, but dealing with goods or services. It can be full-time or part-time, upmarket or downmarket, a pocket-money earner or one for the person who wants to make big money.

Great potential with little risk

It requires little outlay, no staff, no technical expertise and, apart from a typewriter, no special equipment. Furthermore, a great deal of the work can be done at any time, day or night. It is not for everybody but if you fit the matching business, you can make a fortune.

The only downside is time

There is, however, a downside. It is unlikely that a great deal of money can be made overnight. But the real entrepreneur will not be put off. He will start the business in his spare time while carrying on with another job.

Leads galore at no cost

Every week there are countless newspapers and magazines carrying long columns of classified advertisements. The majority of them are placed by people who want either to buy or sell a service or a commodity. The following, taken from the London *Evening Standard* and provincial papers, are perfect illustrations:

Typical examples

1. CAMERAS. Three unused cameras in cases for sale privately. Cost prices total £450. Best offer to:——
2. FUNDS. Large funds are available for most business purposes. Interest rates reasonable. Profit-sharing considered. Minimum £20,000. Write: John Skinner, XYZ Finance Ltd.......
3. ENVELOPES. 20,000 perfect A4 white, best quality for quick sale. Closing-down sale of Tottenham Stationers. Phone with offer:——
4. BICYCLES. Lady's and gent's immaculate Raleigh bicycles for sale to help purchase car. Best offer ——
5. NEW BUSINESS. Ex-company manager wishes to start his own business with enormous potential. Orders already confirmed. Own bank will match redundancy money being invested. Still require loan of £30,000. Share participation offered. Box ——
6. CAMERA. Private buyer wishes to purchase nearly new Minolta or similar-quality camera in perfect condition. Phone —— evenings.
7. BUILDING LAND. 3 acres with industrial planning permission. For sale or joint development. Phone ——

Newspapers provide your business

The above advertisements appeared in three different newspapers and one magazine in the same week. They are typical of thousands that are inserted in dozens of national and local newspapers and a wide variety of magazines. The opportunities appear obvious but this is not yet the time to start your matching business. First you have to plan exactly how you propose to begin, what class of advertisement you intend to answer, the geographical limits you could sensibly cover, the amount of time and money you are prepared to invest. One eighteen-year-old concentrated on bicycles and made himself a steady £30 a week working mostly in the evenings. At the other extreme, a man made redundant in 1970 specialised entirely in providing finance. In his first year he earned over £50,000 and a few years later had his own small bank.

Libraries save money

Self-training need not take more than a week or two, and it is not necessary to spend a small fortune buying loads of papers and magazines to get a clear idea of the potential which the business offers. Visit the local library and go through all the classified advertisements in every paper they have. Make lists of items and services which you believe you would find easy to discuss. Only include those which are likely to earn you a reasonable commission or profit — there is no point noting the number of £10 second-hand prams advertised. Top-quality electric mowers, on the other hand, might well offer an adequate margin.

Districts make a difference

When you have made your lists, visit another library a few miles away and check the advertisements in the local papers for that district. They could be quite different. Readers from poorer districts rarely sell or are able to buy the same goods as their more affluent neighbours.

Once again, good stationery is essential. Apart from your address and telephone number, you could add a telex and fax number. This does not mean that you have to rush out and buy or hire one. There are countless telex and fax agencies prepared to let people quote their numbers, only charging on telexes and faxes sent or received. It could prove useful, and in any case it looks impressive.

Think of a name

You might also prefer to have a trade name. If you cannot think of a suitable one, you could always use the name of your old school, your road or a combination, or make up a name like Network Financial Services. There is no longer any obligation to register a business name.

Buy, rent or borrow a typewriter

If you do not have a typewriter, you may be able to borrow one in the evenings when it is not being used. Try asking local traders. You have a better chance trying to borrow from small firms who might well understand your problem. As a last resort, place the following advertisement in a local newspaper or in the windows of nearby newspaper shops:

CAREFUL USER wishes to hire modern
typewriter evenings or weekends.

If you or a close friend or relative cannot type, then you will simply have to learn the hard way. Most self-made people did just that.

It may be helpful to consider approaches to one or two of the advertisements quoted earlier, which, at first glance, look a little daunting. No.2 is probably a good one to start with. Write or, better, type to Mr Skinner on the following lines:

Suggested follow-up letters

Dear Mr Skinner,
Your advertisement in the *Daily XXX* might well be of interest to me. I would be grateful if you could let me have full details of the funds and the precise terms on which they are offered. At the same time, perhaps you would also advise me of your scale of charges.
Yours very truly,

(Full name)

Obviously, this leads you to reply to advert No.5

Dear Sir,
Your advertisement in the *Daily XXX* could well be of interest to the directors of funds with which we are currently in touch. If you would let us have the fullest details, we would be pleased to submit them.
At this stage, you are under no obligation whatsoever.
Yours very truly,

(Full name)

The time to take advice

All being well, you might now have a willing lender and a keen borrower. If you have no previous experience, this is the most likely point at which you can go wrong. We all know that experience is your best teacher, but there is no point learning the hard way if you don't have to. If you have a solicitor or an accountant, take your proposition to them and they will guide you. Alternatively, fall back on your bank manager. He may not be the greatest negotiator, but he should have a pretty good idea of how to advise you to take the matter further. Your best option might be to put the two parties in touch after you have a *written* agreement from the fund advertiser that he will share his fees with you.

Fix fees and take references

These are likely to be 2-3 per cent of the total amount advanced. Just to be on the safe side, it might be a good idea to ask Mr Skinner for two references, one of them from his bank.

Forget not your solicitor

You must realise that some intermediaries cannot be trusted and you can only protect yourself as well as you can. If you have a solicitor, he may write your fee agreement on your behalf. Some people are more reluctant to swindle a solicitor than a business man.

Advertisement No. 3 refers to an odd job-lot of envelopes. It could be worth asking for a sample. Good-quality envelopes of the size advertised cost the retailer about £38 per 1,000. If you can buy the lot for about £250-£300, it could be worthwhile for you to parcel them up in packs of a hundred each and sell them on to a few small retailers. The chances are, however, that it's a deal to leave to someone less ambitious than yourself.

No. 7 could have real possibilities. First, though, it is essential to find out the precise location of the site. There is no point in pursuing it if it is miles away from water, electricity and human habitation. An industrial development is fine just so long as there are people around to be employed. If it is within reasonable distance of a town, try to obtain as much information as possible regarding the details of the planning permission and the vendors' asking price.

A third of a fee is better than no fee

While waiting for this information, get in touch with a major estate agent specialising in industrial property. It is important that you go to a specialist and not to an agent who may be an expert on residential property but not have a clue on industrial. If you are unable to find the name of an experienced agent, phone the *Estates Gazette* and ask them for a couple of names. When you have these details write a letter along the following lines:

Always in writing

Dear Sirs,
Your name has been given to us by the *Estates Gazette.*
It is possible that we will shortly have full details of a particularly valuable industrial site. It occupies 3 acres near a good residential area with excellent transport facilities.
Needless to add, planning permission has been obtained.

We would be happy to pass this information to you if you would kindly confirm that:
a) You are likely to have clients interested, and
b) That you will grant us one-third of all fees which you receive resulting from this introduction....

You may be assured that they will be interested but, whatever happens, do not part with any information whatsoever until you have protected your potential fees. Reputable firms rarely risk prejudicing their reputations by trying to renege on written agreements. But, as an old wit once remarked, verbal agreements are not worth the paper they're written on. One last word: if you are sure that fees are owed to you, do not waste time listening to excuses as to why they have not been paid. Instruct a solicitor to collect them for you.

Anyone who likes the matching business will not be short of opportunities. The weekly *Exchange & Mart* could easily provide a very good living for any number of conscientious people in the business.

Plan your profit range

It is very important that you calculate the minimum amount of money you would like to make from your efforts. This will help you to decide the areas on which to concentrate. As a guide, the man who made £50,000 in his first year attempted only to operate with propositions that would give him at least one week's income. That may be just a bit ambitious for some, but it certainly worked well for him.

17

MESSENGER SERVICE

A great need

It is surprising that even with an expensive postal service, telex and fax, there are still thousands of firms who use a personal messenger service every day. There are times when the originals of signed documents are required urgently, when competition requires maximum speed, when deadlines have to be met, when medical data needs to be processed without delay, when important letters are too confidential to be passed by fax or telex. These are the times when people value a personal messenger service.

All you need to start

To start a messenger service one needs:
1. A means of conveyance.
2. A means of communication.
3. Clients.

Better than a car

A bicycle is particularly easy to park but it does limit the geographical area to be covered. A small motor cycle or moped is the most satisfactory to start with. They are not usually expensive to hire, but always check the insurance cover. A car could get caught up in traffic jams, and could produce far more parking fines than the business could possibly justify, even though it would enable you to carry more, and larger or heavier parcels.

Keeping in touch

The most practical means of communication is a walkie-talkie, but it would be unwise to purchase one until you are quite certain that you intend to stay in the messenger business. If you are unable to hire one, pay a telephone agency to take messages for you, and keep in contact with it. Maybe not ideal, but it is reasonably efficient and creates a better impression than an answerphone.

Client production

Finding the clients is, of course, the most important part of the business. But it need not be that difficult if you operate in a well-populated area and approach the problem carefully from a strictly commercial angle. It is recommended that the following steps be taken:

Look for a steady business

1. Make a list of the category of customers who are most likely to need your service. They will include: Advertising agents, Public relations consultants, Newspapers, Solicitors, Accountants, Insurance brokers, Architects, Estate agents, Doctors, Dress designers, Printers, Photographers, Chemists.
Hotels can be a particularly good source of business as they fall into a special category, frequently requiring a messenger service to collect rather than deliver parcels.

Your map is essential

2. Buy a local map with large print. Decide that initially you will cover a collection area of, say, three square miles of the city-centre. Study this area very carefully so that you know most of the roads and the routes you would take to reach them.

Produce your own list for nothing

3. With the help of Yellow Pages make a directory of all the people you would like to contact in that area. The number is unlikely to be as large as you might imagine, with the possible exception of Central London.
4. Draft a leaflet which you will arrange to have distributed to, say, 2,000 addresses in the area. The leaflets and their delivery should not cost more than about £70. Your leaflet might be headed 'IMMEDIATE DELIVERY SERVICE'.

Have a minimum charge

5. People who use personal delivery services are really concerned far more with speed than with price. Do not overcharge, but calculate your prices carefully. You must allow for the fact that you will not be kept busy full-time. If you are aiming to make £200 a week, you must calculate your time to produce a minimum of £300 a week. In any event insist on a minimum charge.

Scale of charges

6. It is a business which is unlikely to have any worthwhile spin-off benefits. It is therefore quite reasonable for you to charge more for small parcels than

for letters, and more for larger parcels than you would for small ones. Make sure that your bag is waterproof.

7. In order not to miss an opportunity, let your local competitors know that you are in business. They may well give you work when they are too busy.

8. At some stage, you may consider investing in a small van to carry larger parcels. Of course, you will charge more for this service.

9. Always make certain that your deliveries are signed for.

Remember the rain

Do remember it is an all-weather business. If this is likely to worry you, it is the wrong business for you.

18

THE MOTOR INDUSTRY

A STEADY £300-£400 A WEEK

No training necessary

This is such a vast business, with so many excellent opportunities, that it probably offers more possibilities to more readers than any other industry covered in this book. It is not necessary to be an engineer, or a mechanic, or even to have worked in the motor industry, in order to make a profit from it. The following figures have been collated, from official sources, to illustrate the scope provided by the industry — an industry that, directly or indirectly, employs the largest number of people in the entire country.

Large business potential

In Great Britain, the total number of private cars owned by individuals and companies exceeds 19,700,000, and the figures are rising. Statistics produced by the Government in 1989 showed that there are over 350,000 cars in Cheshire, 270,000 in Hereford and Worcestershire, 2,360,000 in Greater London, 840,000 in East Anglia, and at least 290,000 in small areas like West Sussex. These random examples have been taken simply to illustrate the size and spread of the market. Furthermore, even allowing for all the old wrecks and rusty bangers on the roads, the majority of private car-owners take an interest in their cars. There are no precise figures available, but the large number of clean or fairly clean cars around speaks for itself.

Car valeting

Some people might imagine that washing cars means walking around the streets with a bucket and sponge, hunting down the odd dirty car. This is fine for Boy Scouts, but it is unlikely to develop into a business or even to produce an income commensurate with your needs or the time involved.

Finding the right market

To begin with, it is important to consider how to find and keep sufficient customers. The private home trade might do well at weekends, but most men drive their cars to work or to the local railway station, and it is impractical to expect busy housewives, even if they're not working, to pin themselves down to a specific time every week. The answer is to move into the commercial field. Even the smallest towns have a number of private and public car parks catering for employees and those working locally.

Few people in the business

Car-wash stations have only become a successful business because there are so few people who have taken the trouble or the initiative to provide a highly efficient personal service. The automatic car-wash units which now appear in dozens of towns throughout the country are becoming increasingly more popular even as they become more expensive. Forgetting the charges made by the expensive garages in major cities, even small repair yards outside Solihull, Gateshead and Portsmouth are now charging over £5 for a wash.

Time- saving is a real benefit

In addition, of course, the car-owners have to spend time, patience and petrol driving their cars to be cleaned, as well as waiting in queues. Little imagination is required to appreciate the benefits of having cars carefully cleaned and inspected while their owners are at work. It becomes even more attractive if this service is offered for no more than one would have to pay in a garage. But there simply aren't enough operators to go round.

Establish your position

There are two approaches to be considered. You can arrive at a car park early each day and approach people as they leave their cars. This works, and dozens of cleaners do just that. But how much better it would be to establish yourself as the official car cleaner for the site. This can be achieved by writing to the owners of the site or the private parking area and asking for permission. It is an investment to use good-quality stationery. Your letter, addressed to the company secretary, after you have discovered his name, might be written on the following lines:

A letter with no flannel

Dear Mr Burrows,
Having been made redundant when XYZ closed down their factory, I have decided to establish a car valeting service for the executives and staff of a few companies like your own. My special equipment enables me to operate on terms which compare favourably with those offered elsewhere.
Enclosed are copies of references, which I hope will enable you to give me permission to work in your car park *(or parking area)*. I would gladly attend for an interview if you would find this helpful.
Yours very truly,

(Full name)

Making the right impression

Examples of suitable referees were given in an earlier chapter. To these might be added one from the local mayor, to whom you should write a similar letter to the one written to your Member of Parliament (see page 30). Regardless of your image of a car-washer, if Mr Burrows wishes to see you, make sure your clothes and shoes are clean and your face is shaved. It gives the impression of someone who is proud to be establishing the business he has come to discuss. Remember you are a person offering a highly efficient service, you are not an escapee from a meths colony.

A great investment

Your letter refers to modern equipment, and it is this that is the key to your success. An investment of between £300 and £6,000 will buy you an extremely efficient high-pressure cleaner. These machines are ideal for cleaning cars, engines, motor cycles, terraces, garden gates and garden furniture.

What affects your profit

Now, before you start calculating your profit, do take the following into account:

1. You have to drive to and from the site.
2. You may have to spend time driving to other sites.

3. You need to recoup the cost of the equipment.
4. There are fewer than 240 working days in a year.
5. Of these, a fair number will be too wet to work.
6. Your regular customers will be more concerned with your making a good job of their cars rather than a cheap one.

Bearing all this in mind, if you choose your site carefully you should manage to clean at least twenty-five cars a day. Weather permitting, this could produce a gross income in the region of £500 per week. But remember, it is your personal service that has to be competitive.

Personal service

Greeting a customer cheerfully is good public relations but it cannot be passed off as personal service. In the car valet business, you have got to do far better than that if you want to build an on-going business.

As soon as possible after you start, you should make a second investment to cover two very different important items. Together they will cost you no more than £45.

Personal touch increases income

The first is a tyre pump incorporating a gauge, and the second is a supply of notelets printed with your name, address and telephone number. If you think that a tyre looks a little flat, check it. If you are right, pump it up and leave a note on the windscreen telling your customer that he might have a slow puncture. If a customer has a car with good bodywork but no rubber door-protectors, leave a note suggesting that he fixes a pair to protect his paintwork. You could also offer to get them for him — remember to add on 20 per cent for your trouble. Make a special point of checking the condition of the tyres of every car that you wash; when advising a customer that a tyre is worn, you could also mention the name and address of a local company that can replace it. Do the same if you notice missing hubcaps, rusty exhaust pipes, cracked mirrors or any other defects.

Extra profit

If you have earned a good no-claims bonus on your own motor policy, it could be worth your while, if the additional premium required is modest, for you to ask your broker or insurance company for a letter confirming that your motor policy insures you for driving all other motor vehicles. In this event, have copies of the insurance company letter made and keep the original in a safe place. Showing this copy-letter might well encourage your customers to allow you to take their cars to, for instance, the tyre company. That could earn you another commission in addition to a small charge for the service.

Expansion

Once you have established an adequate number of regular customers, you can start thinking of expansion. Some might consider this almost impossible, but it certainly isn't if you plan it carefully. At this stage, you have two great assets: written authority to work on one or more sites, and a first-class machine. You could take the following steps to increase your business:

Future planning with care

1. Find another site or car park as near as possible to where you are working.
2. Obtain permission to service it.
3. Buy a second cleaning machine.
4. This is the most difficult stage. Find someone who can undertake the same work. However well you know that person, obtain three references, preferably from house-owners, building societies, banks or those more responsible than bar-flies. You are about to trust someone, do not be casual about his or her background. You are seeking a person who can increase your income, share your workload, or double-cross you. At least take every precaution so that you never have to blame yourself if you choose badly. Also bear in mind that housewives might make very good car-cleaners, and may have spare time to work during school hours.

Be careful who you trust

5. The problem now is one of trust. There are people who will continue to give you a percentage of the takings without cheating, but there are few of them. It is testing honesty to the extreme to expect anyone to keep an accurate account of unchecked cash indefinitely. If you suggest a high rental for the machine, a bright assistant will go and buy his own as soon as he can afford it. These machines are rented at anything from £7 a day to £20 a week.

Authority gives security

Your security is the authority given to you to operate the site. It might be reasonable to offer to rent the machine and sub-contract the site for an all-in price of, say, £30 a week. If the second site is sufficiently close, it might be more practical to suggest £6 a day. This leaves less chance for excuses. The amount charged must, however, bear a sensible relationship to the profit which your colleague is going to earn. An average rate of 50 pence a car should be acceptable and will give you your rent of £30, provided that there are sixty additional cars being cleaned every week.

Making a practical deal

Ask a solicitor to draft a letter whereby your sub-contractor agrees to vacate the site immediately if requested to do so. The important thing is to make a fair profit and still keep the charges sufficiently low to encourage the person to be honest. It is always a difficult situation but it has certainly been known to work. If it doesn't, you do not stand to lose very much.

Keeping up standards

6. It is important that your sites are fairly close. In this way you can keep an eye on them and ensure that your colleague is maintaining your high standard of work. There are, of course, other ways of paying an assistant or a colleague but, at the end of the day, you have to rely on people's integrity.

Every car-owner needs protection

Nearly every minute of every day and night, a car is stolen somewhere in England. The competent thief passes on the stolen vehicle, usually with changed number plates, within an hour. A few hours later, even the owner finds it difficult to recognise his own car. Stealing cars is a highly organised, efficient industry which costs insurance companies many millions of pounds every year. It also causes enormous distress and aggravation.

Smashing the car racket

It is not the little car thief who disturbs the police, it is the nationwide network that operates with skill and precision timing. Semi-sophisticated locks and simple alarm systems will deter the amateur, but often present no problem to the professional; he either deals with such methods of protection in a matter of seconds or he moves on to another vehicle. He is a skilled operator who probably served his apprenticeship under a professional when they were doing time together. He has been taught to avoid Rolls-Royces, Ferraris and other cars that are difficult to unload or time-consuming to handle. In the latter category are those cars with their numbers engraved on all windscreens and windows. The professional car-thief knows that speed is the secret of his success and that it is easier to steal an unmarked car than take the trouble to change a complete set of windows.

A small or a major investment

An engraving tool can be purchased for as little as £3, but using it is a long job. The right tool to engrave car numbers on windows can complete the task in just a few minutes.

Finance is easy

Sophisticated equipment for carrying out such jobs quickly and efficiently will cost in the region of £750. This is not cheap, but then people are paying between £8-£10 to have their cars protected in this way. It is a service that many of your car-wash customers and others would appreciate. Marking just two cars a day could earn you an extra

£100 a week. On that basis, it should not be too difficult to convince your bank manager that he would not be gambling by making you a loan. If you do not have a car to carry your machines, hire a small one. You will cover the cost very quickly.

Good business in bad weather

When it is pelting with rain, or the snow is a foot deep, you are out of the car-cleaning business until the weather improves. But you can always offer your window-marking service to garages. You may have to give them a special price but, it is still good business for a wet day.

19

PHOTO
ON
PLATE

A STEADY INCOME EARNER

There are very few businesses which can produce a first-class income from a modest investment. To find one that has considerable potential and yet requires little travelling is rare indeed. This really can be claimed by manufacturers of photo-on-china machinery.

A good business to work from home

The process is so simple and takes barely ten minutes. It is an ideal small business easily operated from home, and, furthermore, it is really not difficult to find enough customers for you to earn a net £60 a day or more. There is a never-ending queue of parents, grand-parents, couples and individuals who would love to have their favourite photograph processed on to a plate or saucer. According to size, the total cost to you would vary between £1.50 and £4.00, depending on the cost of the plates. These can often be bought very cheaply from second-hand furniture and china shops, junk shops, and from small stores offering incomplete dinner sets. Although there is thought to be little demand for people wishing to use their own china, it is a service which can be offered. In such cases a discount of, say, 20 per cent would be reasonable.

Start with under £500

The entire equipment can be purchased for under £500, including VAT; a superior model of photo-on-plate machinery is marketed for around £848 inclusive. There are much cheaper models, but you usually get what you pay for. The machines, which take up little space, are simple to operate and do not require a dark-room.

Check your suppliers

If you have real confidence in the potential of the business, buy the equipment which you know will last. Take a little time to study the literature and, in every case, ask the supplier for at least three names of satisfied customers. A short list of suppliers appears at the end of this chapter.

Marketing should really not be a problem as there are so many people to help you to get established. The following are proven ways of building this lucrative business:

Get the business going

1. Arrange to display samples of your plates in the windows of gift shops, photographic shops, chemists and shops that sell baby goods. Offer to complete all orders within 48 hours and grant the stores a 30 per cent commission. They collect the moneys for you so you will have no bad debts.
2. Check local papers that are not already carrying advertisements for this type of business. Unlike most businesses, with this one you will advertise for agents and not customers. The following may be considered suitable:

Part-time agents

£100 A WEEK COMMISSION
Opportunity for part-time agents

Working your own hours you should earn
at least £100 a week from interesting work.
You use your own initiative and make a little effort
and we show you how to make it and keep on making it.

Do remember that the commission to agents will be in addition to that which you will have to pay to any stores introduced by your agents.
3. Write to head teachers of local schools, who may be prepared to advise their Parents' & Teachers' Associations of your service. It could be well worth your while to offer a special discount of, say, 20 per cent. Just one or two schools could provide a very profitable on-going business.

4. Contact local garages. They are always looking for extra lines, particularly those which take up no space.

5. Approach photographers — they may be prepared to act as agents for you.

Watch your competition

IMPORTANT: Before you consider this business, check the number of shops in your area which are providing the service. If there are already quite a number, do not pursue the matter. It is important not to try to develop a business in a district which is already extensively covered. The exception to this, of course, is if you can be very competitive and still make a good living for yourself.

Equipment suppliers

Manufacturers that specialise in photo-on-plate equipment include Fordways Products, 90 Blackamoor Lane, Maidenhead, Berks SL6 8RH; Pottery Portraits, Anglesey. These names are given for information only. No doubt there are others to be found in the Yellow Pages in different parts of the country.

20

SECURITY SERVICES

Burglary is a growth business

There was a time when only the homes of the rich were attractive to professional burglars, and most petty thieves specialised in pick-pocketing and shoplifting. This period, when the vast majority of people felt that their little treasures and modest possessions hardly merited the attention of ambitious thieves, now seems light years ago. Times have changed. Today burglary is a growth industry; crime pays for over 80 per cent of its practitioners, and high unemployment ensures no shortage of enthusiastic apprentices. Consequently, there are no longer enough rich houses to go round and every home has become a worthwhile potential target for criminals.

Not enough police

In addition, the police force is undermanned, physical assault frequently accompanies a burglary, and judges tend to be more influenced by psychiatrists than by prosecuting counsel. To complete the unhappy picture, overcrowded, understaffed prisons now provide the most conducive environment for the training of criminal graduates.

Endless scope

All this adds up to just one thing. There is unbelievable scope for those who wish to provide security services. From window-locks to alarms, from floodlights to chains, from guard-dogs to sirens, from hidden cameras to barbed wire — there is no end to the list of protective devices which can be installed to help the house-owner protect his home and his family. Anyone choosing to specialise in this area is certain of public support and official encouragement. The business opportunities are endless, as millions of potential customers simply wait to be approached with a practical plan to safeguard their possessions.

Do not hawk

Hawking gadgets, however cheap they might be, is not the way to build a business or a reputation. Security is a professional occupation, and anyone claiming to be an adviser or consultant in this field should behave accordingly. Initial impressions are most important. If you want to project the image of a consultant, remember to behave and dress like one and not like an onion salesman. The place to obtain the most significant information and guidance is where crime and its perpetrators are best understood. The police station.

Take police advice

Nearly every station now has a home security officer. Such men are knowledgeable, experienced and, more often than not, very helpful indeed. Remember that, like the family doctor or the priest, the police are there to serve the public. Contrary to popular belief, they welcome enquiries, they are trained to be supportive, and their specialist staff are pleased to make time for those who seek their assistance.

Keep police informed

The police are recruited from every walk of life, they move in a real world, and they usually have the right answers to your problems. Your first approach might be by telephone to arrange an appointment with the local security officer; alternatively, address the following short letter to him:

Dear Sir,
It is my intention to establish a business providing means of protection against fire and burglary to local householders. Before doing so, I would welcome your advice and the opportunity to discuss my plans with you. With this in view, I will telephone to arrange a mutually convenient appointment.
Yours truly,

(Full name)

Remember references

Before you attend that very important meeting, you should make sure that you have a number of excellent references from responsible people who have really known you well for some time. Ideally, your list should include people like your doctor, your old employer, a solicitor, a police inspector, a Justice of the Peace, a trade union official, the manager of the local football club, a minister of religion, a school teacher, a local counsellor, your Member of Parliament, or other individuals whose occupations are normally identified with being responsible.

Get your facts and figures

Next, write to the main burglar alarm specialists requesting full particulars of their installations. Obviously, you should be completely familiar with the services you are likely to recommend. If possible, visit one or two of them and tell them that you are planning to start an independent security advice service. You could also mention that you would be looking for a commission on all introductions. It is better for you to try to negotiate a modest initial fee and a small share of the annual charges which all these companies make. In this way you will be building an income for yourself.

But there is a great deal more to the security business than being an agent or broker for burglar alarm companies. If you are not an electrician or a competent handyman this business may not be for you. On the other hand, you could always work in partnership with qualified carpenters, electricians or builders.

DIY shops can help

If you do not know any, you will probably find that the manager of your local DIY store is familiar with those in the neighbourhood qualified to help you. Should you decide to use such people, always obtain references from them before you recommend them. Ideally, some of those references should come from satisfied customers.

Word of caution

Never risk recommending someone whose work you are not sure of.

The obvious protections include door- and window-locks, various on-off light systems, spy-holes for front doors, bars for ground-floor windows and, of course, dogs. In addition there are floodlit garden systems, neighbour-communicating alarms, and a number of electronically controlled deterrents.

Before you start

Anyone thinking of starting in the home security business could do well to get into touch with companies providing security packages, but do ask them for references from satisfied customers before advancing any moneys. This is no reflection on the company but it is to remind you that you must always make your checks.

In Chapter 18, mention was made of a machine used to mark car windows. This machine can also be used very effectively to mark such items as television sets, video recorders, clocks, cameras and many other expensive items kept at home.

Unimark is business

With 826,000 cases of burglary a year to prove your case, there can be no shortage of potential customers. The manufacturers issue a number of very useful packs including a list of uses for their marking machine. They also provide very impressive signs for houses where property has been marked by their machines.

You could try distributing a hundred copies of the following letter to the owners of more expensive homes in a given area near to your own home. Your headed paper might well carry a heading such as: 'HOME SECURITY ADVISER'.

A letter of approach

Dear Sir,

Every minute, day and night, a house like yours is burgled. It is invariably an unhappy, disturbing and expensive experience.

When it happens, most people immediately start checking their home security, and only then begin worrying about the action that should be taken to prevent a recurrence.

It is my business to try and help you to beat the burglar the first time. To achieve this I have discussed your potential problem with the local police and the major firms who specialise in this area.

A meeting will give me the opportunity to show you my references and will place you under no obligation whatsoever. Hopefully, it will also avoid distress being caused to you and your family.

Yours very truly,

(Full name)

This is an ideal small business for anyone who is prepared to work hard to earn an above-average income.

21

TOYS

A BUSINESS TO START WITH UNDER £500

Facts about toys

The following facts will enable you to appreciate the size of the British toy industry.

1. The industry produces over four hundred million pounds' worth of toys a year.
2. Over 50,000 people are employed in Britain making and selling toys, games and sports goods.
3. Soft toys alone account for more than £30 million.
4. The industry has its own Association of British Toy and Hobby Manufacturers, operating from 80 Camberwell Road, London SE5 0EG.

This chapter will concentrate entirely on the soft toy side of the business and how to become a part of it.

Ideal for women

The making of soft toys might well be an ideal business for women who enjoy sewing, are imaginative and like the idea of working mainly with other women. This does not exclude men at all, but they are less likely to be associated with the type of handiwork involved.

The guidelines for starting this cottage industry are relatively simple, but carrying them out will require patience, initiative, imagination and persistence. It is a business that can be launched for under £500, and the profits should start rolling in within a matter of weeks.

Produce your first samples

Anyone planning to start in the soft-toy business should be able to make every product they intend to include in their collection. From personal experience you will learn whether a particular toy is too intricate to make to become profitable. In addition, by having a clear idea of time involved, you will be able to calculate your cost price reasonably accurately.

Good books to read

Before you buy the few tools of your new trade, it is suggested that you carefully read as many books on toy-making as you can find. There is no need to buy any as public libraries are full of them. Among the many that are worth studying are:

Favourite Toys by Jean Greenhowe, published by Hamlyn. A delightful book of cuddly toys and toy houses, with many excellent tips.

The Fairytale Doll Book by Valerie Janitsch, published by David & Charles. This is a delightful book full of traditional fairytale figures such as the Three Bears, Little Red Riding Hood and Goldilocks. The book contains details of how to make the dolls plus clothes and furniture to go with them.

Making Glove Puppets by Mary Ford, published by Mary Ford Publications. This contains plenty of ideas for different puppets as well as step-by-step instructions.

Crafty Clowns by Di Campbell, published by David & Charles. This book again contains plenty of ideas and step-by-step instructions.

Making your own Teddy Bear by Peggy and Alan Bialosky, published by Thorsons. The ever-popular teddy bear is a good toy to have in your range. This book gives you ideas for several different versions of the traditional teddy bear.

Dollmaking by E. J. Taylor, published by Aurum. Another useful book with ideas for different dolls.

Market research is important

The last stage before you actually get started is to carry out a little market research. Visit a number of large and small toy shops and make detailed notes of their toys and prices. You might casually enquire which soft toys are the most popular. It is no secret that in 1985 nearly 50 percent of all soft toys sold in Britain were bears of one sort or another. This percentage figure has fallen in recent years to approximately 20 per cent in 1989, due mainly to the huge sales of character products such as Garfield. However, it is still worth investigating the viability of making bears.

Make sure that you comply with the law

The Toys (Safety) Regulations of 1989 are now in force. These require toys to be made in accordance with BS 5665. Also take note of the Consumer Protection Act. Copies of government regulations are available from HMSO and copies of British Standards are available from the Sales Department, BSI, Linford Wood, Milton Keynes MK14 6LE, telephone 0908 221166. Alternatively, copies of British Standards and government regulations are available for reference at most central public libraries.

Also available from BSI Education at Linford Wood, Milton Keynes, is a helpful leaflet entitled *Playtime Soft Toys. Guidelines from British Standards*. Among helpful hints in the leaflet is a list of the British Standards which soft toy makers need to adhere to.

Watch the profit margins

It is important to keep in mind that:
1. Retailers expect to make a 50 per cent profit, which is a third of the selling price. It would therefore be reasonable for you to plan to produce your toys for little more than 35-40 per cent of the retail price, and leaving you a margin of not less than 30 per cent.

Production targets

If the average retail selling price of your toys is £10, you will have to be prepared to sell them to the retailer for no more than £6.50. On that basis your total manufacturing costs should be no more than £4.50, leaving a net profit of £2 per toy. Allowing for odd mishaps and miscalculations, you should aim to make and sell 150-200 toys a week.
2. You will probably have to face the fact that you will be unable to compete with the prices of many imported toys.
3. You will not be able to produce sufficient inexpensive toys to make a good living for yourself.
4. Thousands of people are extravagant when buying gifts for children. Kids do not only have birthdays, they also have Christmas, measles and doting relations.
5. So long as there are children, there will be a toy business.
6. You have great advantages over the big manufacturer. You have very few fixed overheads and you can afford to make for actual orders rather than stock. Furthermore, it will pay you to seek the smaller outlets for sales which your larger competitor cannot afford to do. Referring to Chapter 1, 'Thinking and Observing', this is an excellent time to consider sales opportunities which are likely to be missed by others.

Back to Main Street

Walking down from Main Street, there are two possibilities on the left-hand side and two on the right. The greetings-card shop might well be delighted with a new line. There must be many customers who buy cards for children there. They could carry a few toys without having to worry about space. A shop like Next might possibly like the odd toy for window-dressing. It is worth taking trouble over such an order as it could lead to worthwhile business from that group.

Why travel agents?

On the other side are the estate agents with their uninteresting window, and the travel agents. The former might only require a limited number for effect, but the latter might find it a useful item to sell to parents taking children abroad. As far as possible you should try to have different toys in each shop. 7. It should be a business to enjoy and not just to produce an adequate income.

Now to your investment. You will need:

* Three pairs of scissors: a long-bladed pair for cutting out your material, a small pair for cutting yarn and for trimming, and a third pair for cutting paper. Do remember that a good pair of scissors can easily become blunt from cutting paper.
* A ruler and a meter stick. You will need these for marking and for measuring.
* Needles. A good selection, bearing in mind that you will need different needles for different types of thread, for pulling thread through stuffing, and those with blunt points used for joining pieces of knitting. Knitting needles and darners will prove useful.
* A tape measure.
* Glue suitable for fabric. Sticky tape. A good supply of various types of paper as used by a dressmaker, including tracing paper, graph paper and ordinary paper for templates.
* A sharp craft knife for cutting cardboard.
* Finally, fine and medium paint-brushes for painting on the toys themselves.
* A selection of coloured cottons, and perhaps also heavy thread for tougher materials.

Buying materials cheap

* Material. This very important item has intentionally been left till last. It could be a worthwhile exercise to go round stores like Marks & Spencer and Littlewoods, all companies included in the list on page 157. They each have dozens of suppliers manufacturing cotton and woollen goods. The off-cuts from these factories are often swept into sacks for the dustmen. When you have decided on the materials that would be most useful to you for stuffing, little can be lost by writing to the chairman of these large stores along the following lines.

Try a letter

Dear Mr X,
Your reputation for assisting the unemployed is well known. Having been made redundant recently, I feel the time is opportune for me to start my own small enterprise and I have chosen the toy business.
In this connection I will require suitable materials for stuffing, and it occurs to me that many of your suppliers may well have off-cuts complying with

BS1425 which I would find extremely useful. I wonder if you could kindly advise me of any companies whom you feel might be helpful to me.

When replying I would be most grateful if you would let me know if I may mention your name when writing to the manufacturers you recommend.

Thanking you in anticipation of your kind assistance.

Yours sincerely,

(Full name)

Check local suppliers

Other suitable materials, like cardboard, miniature bottles and paper, might be obtained by writing to major chain stores like Sainsbury's, Boots or Northern Foods. The worst that can happen is that some of them will not respond. It is certainly worth trying. While waiting for your replies you could check whether there are any local manufacturers in your locality who would allow you to collect off-cuts from them.

No shortage of staff

While gathering all your requirements, you will have time to recruit your staff, following the procedure suggested on pages 49 and 62. You can expect a large response to your advertisements from middle-aged and elderly ladies who have considerable needlework experience. Others who may be less competent might well be retained for cutting patterns and less exacting work. Before you see any of them you should decide which toys you are going to make initially. Studying the books mentioned earlier should give you a very clear idea of those toys which can be produced in sufficient numbers to give your outworkers adequate financial reward. They will be employed on piece-work, and it is important that they find their pay worth their effort. Do remember that little children are thrilled by toys which they can play with as well as love. If you decide to make a rabbit, you might include a detachable scarf for cold weather or a hat for special occasions. A daddy rabbit could have a pair of denims, a mummy rabbit an apron, and a baby rabbit a pinafore. They could each have their own nightdresses and pyjamas. These little colourful extras are easy to make and should help to sell your products. But do work out the additional cost carefully and then check with one or two retailers that they would find such toys easy to sell at the higher prices.

Keep to safe materials

A WORD OF WARNING. Do not use any materials which could possibly injure or damage the health of a child, e.g. pins, glass eyes, buckles, safety-pins, paint containing lead, etc. Several of the books mentioned make specific reference to the safe materials which can be used. In this connection do make sure that you have effected adequate insurance.

Costs and Value Added Tax

Check your costs very carefully before quoting your prices. These should include an item for materials which may at first cost you nothing, as there could come a time when you will have to buy them. Also, do not forget to check the position regarding VAT.

Beware of large customers

Finally, as you will be providing attractive hand-made toys at competitive prices, do not give credit. Having a large customer is no good to you if he keeps you waiting for your money. Too many of them have been responsible for putting small manufacturers out of business. You are planning to enter the soft-toy business and you simply cannot afford to include banking in your service.

Your Own Agencies

This section is concerned with agency businesses which do not require support from principals or suppliers of goods or services.

Those considering this class of enterprise are advised to check whether they are wise — or obliged — to carry special insurance protection.

22

BABY-SITTING

The majority of normal, intelligent people of almost any age can make very satisfactory baby-sitters. In the absence of any special circumstances, one only needs to be sure that the TV isn't pitched louder than the baby and that one has a telephone number for an emergency. The demand for this service from most sections of society will certainly remain constant. Even those with little spare money for any lavish entertainment take an evening off occasionally to visit a relative or a friend, a cinema or a pub.

Parents have preferences

Of course, there are exceptions, but the majority are not really happy being dependent on the little girl next door. Most parents are quite convinced that their children are different from all others, and are often desperate to find a really reliable baby-sitter. A bright fourth-former is all right, but, for many, not ideal.

Some like older people

Whether their thinking is right is not important. They are the potential clients for whom you hope to cater. The fact remains that an older person is often considered more responsible.

Check local demand

If a little research in your district confirms that there is a demand, you could be all set to establish a baby-sitting agency. Before you rush into the business you should:
* Speak to parents and tradesmen in your neighbourhood and find out how they manage for baby-sitters.
* Check whether they think that a reliable service would be appreciated.

Personal experience important

* If you or your wife have never baby-sat for strangers, it would be a practical move for you each to obtain some experience. You would then have a clearer idea of what people expect and also how responsible and courteous they are.

The secret of making a success of this business is preparation. The following points should serve as a guide for setting up and operating your service:

Qualifications required

* First, it is necessary to decide precisely what baby-sitting service you are going to provide, and to whom. It is important that you ascertain whether or not parents require sitters with different skills: although the majority may only need a sensible person to sit in for a few hours, some might be much happier with a mother who is familiar with changing nappies and relieving babies' wind.

Check your costs

* Although one would rightly imagine that not a great deal of start-up capital is required, it is still sensible to make some estimate of expenses to enable you to recognise the potential of the business. As you will be operating from home, your major additional costs will be your telephone, stationery, travelling and advertising.

In business for under £300

If no one is there to man your telephone all day, it could be worth buying an answerphone for about £70. Your stationery will, to start with, be restricted to your headed paper, and possibly a small leaflet, so you are unlikely to need more than £100 to cover this very adequately. Travelling may not be considered a major item, but for reasons explained below it will be a real overhead and you might allow a sum like £60 for the first month. Newspaper advertising is far too expensive for this type of business in the early stages. You will therefore be dependent on cards in newsagents' and shops' windows, and leaflet distribution. Again, £50 a month should be more than sufficient for the former, and £40 a month for the latter. It is therefore reasonable to estimate that, in addition to higher telephone bills, the agency could be comfortably launched for £260-£360.

Do keep a map

There are two further items which could help your business enormously. One is a local map to make you familiar with the neighbourhood and to help you to decide which baby-sitter would be most conveniently placed for which client. The other item is a second telephone.

Have two phones

This will enable you to speak to your client and your baby-sitter at the same time when fixing appointments.

You may have to register

* Before doing anything else, check with your local Social Services Department whether or not you are obliged to register. This is extremely important in order to ensure that you are not infringing the law in any way. For example, it is illegal to care for children for more than 2 hours a day, or 10 hours a week for reward unless you are a registered child-minder. This condition does not apply to blood relatives. In any event, your local Social Services Department can probably offer you good advice. Take it.
* You should also check with your local authority as to whether you require a licence to operate the employment agency. Do not leave this to chance as it could result in your being prosecuted and having your business closed down. This is quite separate from your discussions with the Social Services Department.

What to charge

* Then ascertain the maximum hourly rate that is being paid by the better-off in your area. You are not going to compete on price, only on service.
* If the average sitter takes £7 an evening, you as agent are entitled to £2.33 — a third of the fee. This might not seem a lot, but fifty or sixty sitters, working two or three evenings a week, could make a very useful business for anyone. And it doesn't have to stop there. It could open up many other opportunities. You might well develop the agency to provide several other services — but more of this later.

A responsible family business

* Right from the beginning you must be clear in your own mind that you are starting a responsible family service which you are going to operate on firm business principles. You not only want to keep every client, you also hope that each one will be pleased to talk about you favourably. They should be your greatest advertisements.
* Remember, there is no point rushing around looking for customers until you are properly organised.

Draft your adverts with care

As recommended in the last of the above points, your first shop-window advertisement should be for baby-sitters and not for clients. It should be short and to the point. The copy might well be the following:

XYZ PROFESSIONAL BABY-SITTING SERVICE

Responsible baby-sitters required for Bolton Cross area. Preference will be given to mothers, nurses and others with experience. Good rates of pay and regular work. References will be required. Telephone:——

XYZ PROFESSIONAL BABY-SITTING SERVICE

Take no chances with your staff

When you receive enquiries, you should insist that you call on them. A visit to their homes can tell you a great deal about their attitudes to cleanliness, tidiness and children.

The fact that you have taken this trouble will always make a good impression on your clients. Without being unduly pedantic in your selection, it must always be remembered that you are seeking intelligent, practical and responsible people. Those with domestic or nursing experience or the wives of teachers, policemen, doctors, social workers, and others accustomed to a disciplined routine tend to be very reliable. Whoever they are, always take two references, preferably from previous employers who have known the applicant for at least five years. Also obtain a completed application form from each potential employee. This form can be run off by your local photo-print shop and should not cost more than 10p a copy. The following might well serve as a practical questionnaire:

A good questionnaire is the most important start to your business

1. Name
2. Address
3. How long living in area
4. Date of birth
5. Married/Single/Divorced
6. Ages of children, if any
7. Home telephone number
8. Work telephone number
9. Occupation
10. Occupation of husband
11. Any special training, e.g. nursing, teaching etc.
12. Times available
13. Are weekends convenient/inconvenient?

14. State of health
15. Names, addresses and telephone numbers of two referees

Signature.. Date ....
For official use only ....
(here you make your own notes indicating the impression the applicant made on you.)

Do not have doubts

Completion of this form will not only give you all the facts you need but will also show applicants that they are dealing with an efficient firm. Always check references, and if you have any doubts at all, do not offer work to this applicant. Apart from any distress you might cause by recommending an irresponsible person, you might also prejudice your own reputation.

When you interview each applicant just imagine that you are considering them to look after your own child or a child you know. You must do your best to cover the following points:

A check-list for your interview

1. Does the applicant appear intelligent?
2. Does the applicant have any knowledge of first aid?
3. Would the applicant know what to do in an emergency?
4. Has the applicant experience in dealing with babies and young children?
5. Will the applicant appreciate that they are not allowed to invite friends without authority?
6. Can the applicant be relied upon to report unreliable clients, e.g. those who arrive home much later than agreed, those who drink excessively and others who behave badly?

While waiting for your enquiries, you can be having your leaflets printed. Again these should be written in clear, short sentences, as follows:

XYZ PROFESSIONAL BABY-SITTING SERVICE

Our responsible baby-sitting service includes among its employees many parents with experience of dealing with youngsters of every age. Every baby-sitter employed has been interviewed and has provided first-class references. Special terms for regular clients.
XYZ PROFESSIONAL BABY-SITTING SERVICE
22, Whittington Crescent, Bolton Cross
Telephone:——

Your 'special terms' could be a discount of 10 per cent where, say, a client requires a baby-sitter on a given day every week for more than a month, or some variation on this theme.

When you receive enquiries, always ask:

The second check-list

1. The number of children.
2. Do they have an emergency number where the sitter can make contact if necessary?
3. Their telephone number. This is important. Always ring back to check that the number is genuine. Also check it in the telephone directory. Although some people are ex-directory, the vast majority are not and it is just a precaution to ensure that the address and the telephone number tally.

Protect your sitters

If you have any doubt about the caller, make a journey to the address and check it. This is part of the service that you provide to the sitter.
4. Do make it clear that you expect clients to drive sitters home at night if the sitters have not got their own transport.

To begin with do not order more than 2,000 leaflets. This should be sufficient to get the agency going. Before placing your order, approach a well-established plumber, electrician, veterinary surgeon, garage and car-hire service. Explain to them that you have established your agency, and would be producing leaflets to include the names of a limited number of established local firms

Extra income

Your modest charge for this direct introduction to potential customers would be £20 a quarter. This will not only cover all the costs of printing and distribution, it could also give you a very handsome profit. This directory, which you may decide to print down one side of your leaflet, can also include businesses which do not fall into the emergency category but are very useful numbers for most householders. They might include builders, gardening services, car dealers, florists, hairdressers, shoe repairers, the local gift and baby-wear shops, and any others you can interest. Payment should always be a quarter in advance, but before you decide on the amount, you could discuss it with your bank manager or one of the local tradesmen with whom you are friendly. Rates will vary from district to district, and whilst one does not want to undercharge, there is no point in fixing rates which are not likely to be accepted.

Letting people know

Every baby-sitter will be given a small supply of your leaflets to give to each client, and you might be able to persuade a few shops to carry them near the tills. Send a few to the local clergy, headmasters, secretaries of womens' guilds and clubs, local libraries, childrens' health clinics, GPs, and anyone who is ever likely to be asked if they know a reliable baby-sitter. You might also try to persuade the managers of cinemas in the district that it could be in their interest to have some of your leaflets near the ticket desk. In addition, check your Yellow Pages for a firm of leaflet distributors who will operate in your neighbourhood. They charge about £16 per 1,000 leaflets if your leaflet is distributed on its own. The cost is likely to go down to a sum like £9 per 1,000 if your leaflet is distributed with a group of others. If they choose their roads carefully, they can produce some excellent clients. A 3 per cent response could give you thirty new on-going clients for only £16

Do not tolerate bad payers

When it comes to collecting payment, keep your system as simple as possible. Make it the responsibility of the client to pay the baby-sitter each time they sit. Having kept a clear record of every booking in a large diary, you arrange for every sitter to send you 30-35 per cent of their fee immediately after they have been paid. Never give credit to a client or a baby-sitter; if you encounter a bad payer simply make a note never to do business with that person again. It is cheaper and less strain on your nerves to deal with such matters as quickly as possible.

Plan expansion slowly

Once the business is running satisfactorily, increase the number of shop-window advertisements. Keep careful records that will tell you which advertisements are producing customers from the more prosperous areas. These are the clients who are most likely to appreciate other services which you can develop, such as daily helps, temporary nurses, holiday nannies, shopping and walking companions for the elderly, and possibly part-time secretaries. But, one service at a time. In each case your prime objective must be to plan carefully in order to build and maintain a good name as well as a profitable business. This business could be producing a very good income indeed within only a few months.

Always cover your liability

Finally, a word of caution: make it clear to all your clients that you accept no liability whatsoever for losses or breakages caused by any of your sitters. Nevertheless, endeavour to obtain whatever liability insurance can be effected for modest premiums.

23

CHILD-MINDING

A very different business

This is a very different business from baby-sitting. In the first place, you are obliged by law to register with your local Social Services Department. In the second place, it is a limited exercise, as child-minders are only allowed to have up to three children including their own. However, unless you are a registered child-minder it is illegal to care for children for more than 2 hours a day, or 10 hours a week, for financial gain. This does not include blood relatives.

Time to get started

Furthermore, unlike a baby-sitting agency, it could take as long as six months for your registration certificate to come through. Once registered, however, the child-minder is allocated an adviser who is readily available to help with problems.

This relatively modest business is best suited to a responsible mother who feels capable of looking after up to three children including her own, someone who can stand noise and is not obsessively tidy.

A good support business

It will never become a great enterprise but it could produce a net income of around £50 a week per child looked after, and might be a very useful exercise to help the family finances while the father of the house is, say, building his own new business. One successful child-minder confided that the profits enabled her family to have good holidays instead of no holidays.

Child-minding is a very responsible, demanding and exacting undertaking. It is best considered by women who genuinely love children and have a natural ability to cope with them. Those who believe that they could happily accept such a challenge will not have to learn everything about it the hard way, though.

Your own association

Fortunately, there is The National Childminding Association (8 Masons Hill, Bromley, Kent BR2 9EY). They are a responsible organisation who assist many thousands of professional child-minders to do a first-class job. Their publications, which are modestly priced, are a must for anyone contemplating this business.

Extending into related areas

Of course, an enterprising person could eventually extend the business to a nursery group. Again, one is required to register with the local authority Social Services Department. They would probably be influenced by experience and qualifications: someone who is a qualified nursery nurse, for instance, or has taught in a junior school may well be considered highly suitable compared to those with no training whatsoever. Advice can be sought from the British Association for Early Childhood Education (111 City View House, 463 Bethnal Green Road, London E2 9QY).

Is this business really for you?

If you are impatient, house-proud or short-tempered, do not give this chapter a second thought. If you would like a much clearer picture of what is entailed before you make up your mind, buy a copy of *The Childminder's Handbook,* an excellent handbook produced by The National Childminding Association.

24

CLEANING SERVICES

The part-timers

For many years, housewives, students, resting actors and actresses, artists, philosophers and others have found it practical and relatively rewarding to undertake cleaning jobs. The hours are not usually too demanding, the pay is reasonable for the work, and the obligations are limited. It appeals to people in categories such as those mentioned above because part-time work of this kind enables them to cope better financially with their main interests while giving them time to pursue them.

It is a little surprising that so many in this large labour force operate independently. Of course, it does have moonlighting attractions, but few would in any case be seriously affected by tax considerations, particularly as many direct employers tend to pay less specialised agencies.

The cleaning agency

The very nature of the work provides numerous opportunities for operating a successful cleaning services agency. Contrary to popular belief, the domestic front is not the best field in which to operate. Collecting moneys creates many problems and, worse still, a large percentage of housewife-employers tend to forget their loyalty to the agency. Cleaning services can work profitably in this sector but it seems to involve far more hassle than it does in commerce.

Why companies prefer agencies

Companies and business men readily accept that bills have to be paid promptly if they want the service to continue, and, more important, the amount of money involved is not sufficiently important for them to offer agency staff direct employment. They prefer to have a reliable firm to take care of this responsibility, a firm that is not dependent on the whims, ailments or family problems of an individual cleaner.

Staff your first priority

In some ways the preliminaries for setting up such a firm are not dissimilar to those for a baby-sitting service. Recruiting follows very much the same method, except that the geographical area covered is likely to be much larger. Consequently, you will be obliged to spread your shop-window advertisements. Furthermore, you are likely to have higher travelling and postage expenses as you will certainly have to visit your commercial clients initially, and then from time to time. To obtain their business you will either make direct calls to business and office premises or write to them. Either way, the immediate response is likely to be slow but, as will be shown a little later, steps can be taken to generate business more quickly.

Having lined up your little army of cleaners and obtained satisfactory references from all of them, you are ready to approach your first customers. This is assuming, of course, that you have already had your visiting cards and leaflets printed.

Unsociable hours

Each time you step into a shop, an office or a factory tell yourself that you are not about to ask for business, you are offering someone an important, first-class service. Most of your customers will want their premises cleaned early in the morning or after working hours in the evening. Calculate your costs to ensure that you can pay your staff well and still leave yourself 25 per cent of the gross income. If you decide to write to a number of firms, you may need to pay a secretarial services company. In the long run this could be a cheap way of dealing with such letters, as such a company is likely to have a word-processor which can produce first-class letters without errors and with comparatively little effort. Your letter addressed to the firm or to the company secretary might well read as follows:

Use a typing agency

Dear Sir,
This firm specialises in providing a professional cleaning service for companies like your own. Unlike other similar businesses we offer:
* Experienced cleaners all of whom are bonded.
* We operate between 6 a.m. and 8 p.m.
* We use the most modern hygienic equipment to ensure that the highest standards of efficiency and cleanliness are always maintained.
* Every contract is checked regularly by a director.
* Our fees are commensurate with our service.
An early appointment could well be in our mutual interest.
Yours very truly,

(Full name)

Always state facts correctly

It is imperative that you ascertain that you are in a position to offer the services which you claim. You must check that some of your potential employees are prepared to work the hours stated. You should also enquire from a reputable insurance company, like Norwich Union or Sun Alliance, exactly what insurance you should have for your business. Third-party cover is essential, but you may not feel obliged to effect fidelity insurance. This virtually protects you and your clients against the dishonesty of your staff. This point should be considered very carefully. Whatever you decide, do not commit yourself verbally or in writing until you are quite sure of the precise cover you wish to effect.

Check the machinery

New sophisticated cleaning machines and materials are constantly being introduced to the market. Make sure that you are familiar with them and if you cannot afford to buy, hire or lease such equipment, do not give the impression that you do. You will be found out all too soon.

Research Yellow Pages

Your first list of addresses might well be taken from the Yellow Pages. While waiting for a response you could check the standards of cleanliness at the local cinemas, public lavatories, libraries and restaurants, many of which frequently have difficulty with cleaning staff. The timing of your inspections might be fortunate. In any event, do let the local town clerk know that your firm is available for contract work in the neighbourhood.

Having covered this area, make a note of every well-sited shop that appears to be to let. Write to the agents and suggest that their new tenants would find your service of interest. This should be good news for the agent to pass on. As soon as you notice the 'Let' sign, contact the agent again and ask for the name of the tenant to whom to write. This is the business on which you should concentrate, as shops and offices like to keep the same cleaner if only for security reasons.

Always check references

In an effort to generate more business, you could place a shop-window advertisement for 'Livewires' — people prepared to do the legwork to find you new clients. Again, check their references regardless of the appearance of the individuals or the stories you are told. Not long ago a very presentable, well-spoken man applied for the job of debt-collector, claiming to have been abroad for many years. In the event it transpired that he had not long finished a seven-year jail sentence. If you find the right man or woman, rehearse their approach with them. You may be able to teach them something or even learn a trick or two yourself.

A one-month trial is long enough

If they are good business-producers, you will know within the first week. Unless they are introducing a flow of business, however small, within four weeks, terminate your agreement. You simply cannot afford to have a no-good going around town using your name. On the other hand, if your Livewires are good, remunerate them well. They could become the backbone of your business. As you will only be paying them on commission, you can afford to give them a generous percentage of your profit for a period of, say, four to eight weeks. Whatever the amount, make sure that it is enough to encourage the individual to continue making an effort on your behalf. Whatever happens, never let go of a good producer who has performed really well. So long as your personalities do not clash, such a person could make good partner material.

Recognise partner material

But, before making any promises or rushing into any commitment, discuss the idea with a solicitor. There are many considerations to be taken into account, none of which should be treated lightly.

Use your bank

The capital required to start this business needs to be planned very carefully. Although you are likely to be paid monthly in arrears, in practice this will be nearer to six weeks than four. Still, your bank manager, knowing the calibre of your clients and the length of their contracts, should be happy to finance your venture so long as it appears to be potentially profitable. This is really just the kind of account that banks are begging for — little risk of loss and real potential. If, by chance, your bank manager is not particularly helpful or is over-patronising, do not worry. There are many other banks and they are mostly looking for new business.

You can start this business with £500

Allowing for the unfinanced percentage of your staff overheads, printing, advertising, travelling, telephone and hire charges, you should be able to get going with a capital of between £500 and £1,000, depending on the margins you allow yourself. Your actual monthly overhead, once your business is launched, will relate largely to the numbers of employees. You are likely to need contracts to clean a medium-sized office building and about thirty shops to make a reasonable living. That should not take too long to achieve, particularly with the assistance of even a reasonably good Livewire. After that, you are in business.

25

HOME & GENERAL SERVICES

This is another chapter where the reader is presented with the idea of providing a service direct to the consumer. It is a field where you can operate alone or, alternatively, build up a labour force: the decision must rest with you after you have considered your financial needs and abilities. In any event, it should be appreciated that in the absence of personal recommendations good references are essential.

Security is your first priority

Apart from requiring efficiency and courtesy, any housewife or other employer will understandably be concerned with security, and they are likely to be interested in your references as well as those of anyone you employ.

Daily help demand has grown

There was a time when daily help was only employed by the privileged financial classes. This is no longer the case. Today, numerous housewives with all types of skills prefer to take jobs rather than spend half their days cleaning their homes. In a world of equal pay and opportunities large numbers of women no longer believe that their place is in the home — at least not all day. Many earn high salaries and are more than happy to spend part of them paying for home help. This has created more opportunities for part-time domestic help than ever before. Conversely, there are others who love to spend time at home, or who are obliged to because of young children or elderly parents. They are to be found in all walks of life — among them are the wives of policemen, servicemen, teachers and underpaid executives — they are interested in taking on regular part-time work, and they do not consider it demeaning to assist in cleaning the homes of others. With the rising standards of living and the increasing demands of children, mothers of all classes are perfectly prepared to undertake a few hours of domestic work a week. This enables many to have their own cars, to provide for holidays, school fees and other family benefits which used to be considered luxuries. An earlier chapter deals with operating a baby-sitting agency. The principles applied are almost identical except that the domestic cleaning business should be more profitable — for strangely enough, people are prepared to pay a far higher rate to those who polish their floors than to those who take care of their children. Of such facts are myths, farces and tragedies created.

Combining two businesses

There is, of course, no reason why you two should not combine a baby-sitting agency businesses with a domestic and commercial cleaning agency and simply call it 'home and general services'. While baby-sitting is obviously for a limited market, cleaning is not. Just consider that, apart from thousands of homes, every shop, office and factory has to be cleaned.

People often prefer firms

Business people rarely clean their own premises; few can even remember the day when a member of their staff last swept a floor. This attitude may be symptomatic of the times we are living in, but, more significant, it is good for the cleaning business. What is more, people like to know that a reliable firm is taking the responsibility for cleaning their premises, rather than an individual who may be obliged to let them down from time to time. Small firms are very often preferred because the principals themselves tend to take a personal interest.

Whether you are working yourself or employing staff, you should charge home-cleaning customers on an hourly rate. You can expect to earn a commission on your staff ranging from 20 to 30 per cent. This should, however, be seen in the light of additional services which your agency might provide; details of such interesting possibilities are covered later in this chapter. Charges to businesses should be calculated on a monthly basis. It will be up to you to assess the time which you believe an *average* cleaner will take and make your charges accordingly.

Do it yourself first

There is no teacher like experience, and you would be well advised to undertake one or two cleaning jobs yourself before employing others. It would be reasonable to allow at least a 25 per cent gross profit. In addition, the following should be taken into account:

Extra profit

1. Small business customers will probably be happy for you to accept responsibility for buying cleaning materials to be kept on their premises. It is simply one less headache for them to think about. In such cases, check the prices of cleaning materials in large cash & carry warehouses against those in local shops. There is no reason why you should not charge your customer the full retail price as you are doing them a service. This could also make a profit of at least 20 per cent in most instances.

Watch your liability and your agreements

2. Despite the fact that you will always take at least two references from each employee, you must consider the liabilities for which you could be held responsible. Accidents to people and property can happen and you don't want the distress or aggravation of having an uninsured claim made against you. The limits of your liability should be expressed very clearly in your letters of agreement.

Use insurance

Your local solicitor should be able to advise you on the wording of your literature, and on the insurance cover which you would be wise to effect. Listen to him carefully, take his advice and do not begrudge his fees: they are part of your investment in your new business. It is at this stage that you obtain quotations from insurance companies or brokers. Insurance can be expensive and there is no point in effecting cover in excess of your legal liabilities.

Long-term contracts

3. Once the business begins to move, build up your reserve of cleaners so that you are ready for the big customer. In addition to areas already mentioned, profitable long term contracts can be obtained from cinemas, government offices, and town clerks. Train yourself to be observant. Carry a small notebook with you in which to record any premises that appear dirty or unswept. Many public lavatories are notoriously unclean, particularly those without attendants on duty. A large number of cleaners will not wish to undertake this work, but those who do will expect, and be entitled to, a higher rate of pay. With the larger account or government contract, always endeavour to secure as long a termination notice as possible. This will enable you to treat your staff well and also give you time to find other contracts without losing your workforce.

Recruit Livewires

4. Do not start this business until you have carefully calculated how much you hope to make from it and in what time. You may have to be a working principal

until you build up your income. Remember also that 'Livewires', referred to earlier in this book, are definitely worth considering for this business too.

Either independently, or as part of your cleaning enterprise, there is a very good, on-going business to be developed in providing a real home-valet service. The vast majority of homes rarely give their carpets and upholstered chairs a thorough cleaning; even offices, showrooms and small hotels, which are vacuumed daily, do little to remove the accumulated dirt from their furniture and furnishings.

A good machine needed

It would be virtually impossible to attempt to earn an adequate income from furniture-valeting without a modern spray-extraction machine designed for the purpose. These vary in height between one foot and three feet. It follows that the only way to transport one of these, whatever size you choose, is by car or van. Prices for machines vary, starting at about £600, but one really does get what one pays for. The smaller machines are very satisfactory for ordinary housework, but larger machines enable one to undertake contracts from hotels, hospitals and large showrooms and business premises.

Buy or lease your machine

Check your Yellow Pages for local companies who supply this type of equipment. It is also a good idea to check with the suppliers if the machines can be leased, rather than bought. This obviously keeps overheads down to a minimum for anyone just starting in business. In addition, the price of the machine includes a training programme by experienced professionals.

£8 an hour plus

The business potential for home valeting is enormous. Furthermore it is continual: house-proud people like to have their homes well-cleaned and kept that way. Your charges should reflect the income you aim to earn plus 30 to 50 per cent to cover your travelling and other material expenses, plus an amount towards the cost of your machine. If you are aiming at making a profit of, say, £50 a day, do calculate your charges at £8 per hour to allow for expenses. Should you be obliged to stretch your working day to get the job done, calculate your charges at £9-10 per hour for overtime. Of course, you do not want to price yourself out of a job and it may be as well to check the going rate in your particular district.

Examine opportunities

If it is too low, try to obtain your work from homes in a better district. Failing that, simply decide that you cannot afford to undertake home valeting and switch entirely to the commercial market. Here, you will find that most firms are more concerned with efficiency and prompt service than with cutting a few pounds off a quotation.

Your own notepaper

Cinemas, shops, showrooms and offices are all good potential customers. As your approach will probably be by letter, you should either put your name on the letterhead followed by 'The Steam Vacuum Valeting Service', or simply use your business name. Your letter might be written along the following lines. (Always find out the name of a manager, partner or director so that you can write a personal letter.):

A letter approach

Dear Mr Humphrey,

My firm specialises in providing a high-powered, hygienic valeting service for large and small companies concerned with maintaining spotlessly clean carpets and furnishings.

Using the most modern equipment, we are able to vacuum-clean up to 80 square metres of carpet per hour. This enables my firm to keep its charges low and quote competitive rates for contract work.

In the course of the next few days I will telephone your secretary in the hope of arranging a convenient appointment.

Yours sincerely,

(Full name)

Should you be approaching any company or subsidiary of a company included in the list on page 157, the following alternative letter should be addressed to one of its directors personally.

A special letter approach

Dear Mr Humphrey,

Your company's well-known concern for the unemployed prompts me to write to you.

Having been made redundant recently I have decided to take this opportunity to start my own business in the field of hygienic vacuum-steam cleaning. *(Then continue as above).*

The response may be less enthusiastic than you expect. This simply means that you have to persevere and look for additional opportunities. You could revert to 'Livewires' (see page 120), or consider the type of individuals or companies who might be pleased to recommend you.

Carpet shop potential

An approach to the managers of carpet shops could well be worthwhile. It would not be difficult for them to advise their customers that your hygienic cleaning process extends the life of good carpets. Furthermore, if they really want to be helpful, they could give you the names and addresses of customers to whom they supplied carpets during the last two or three years. It would be wise at first to restrict the geographical area where you operate, as you could otherwise spend too much time travelling. In order to encourage support from carpet dealers, you should offer to show them the draft of your proposed letter, which will not only bring your name to the attention of the customer but will also serve to remind him of the name of the carpet retailer. It might read as follows:

Dual use of letter

Dear Mrs Brown,
The XYZ Carpet Company has suggested that I write to you.
My firm specialises in providing a hygienic vacuum-cleaning service which prolongs the texture, appearance and life of good carpets and furnishings.
Using the most modern equipment, we are able to keep our costs low and provide a regular service which is interesting many houseproud people like yourself.
We would welcome the opportunity to demonstrate our process and give you a quotation without any obligation.
Yours sincerely,

(Full name)

A two-way business

You could mention that you will telephone for an appointment, but this should be cleared with the carpet shop first. They may prefer you not to push their customers too hard. In return for introductions you could undertake to advise the manager if some of the carpets you see justify replacement: this free reciprocal service could help cement your relationship.

Following up signs to new clients

Another lead to good business could be the signs which builders and decorators display outside the houses and shops where they are working. We all know the mess that such work produces. This provides a golden opportunity to approach owners and tenants to suggest that they might like to have their carpets cleaned immediately after the work is completed. You might even reach an agreement with an enterprising firm of builders who would be prepared to include your cleaning services in their quotation. This might justifiably enhance their reputation for carrying out first-class work efficiently. After all, your fees would be absolutely nominal compared with the costs of decorating and building.

Remember the newspapers

Newspaper advertisements can also lead you to a steady flow of business. Most local weekly and evening papers carry regular advertisements from landlords wishing to let furnished premises. A letter might well encourage some of them to give their accommodation a thorough cleaning between tenants, which is likely to help them to re-let the premises as there's nothing that puts people off more than stained carpets and grubby curtains.

New houses help

With many people having bought their own homes there will be a demand for your services. Effort and consistently obliging service must pay off.

Start with just £100

If you already have some means of transport, this profitable business could be started for little more than £100.

26

TEACHING

PROVIDING THE ANSWERS

Lots of problems are good for businesses

There can rarely have been a time this century when there have been more problems in the teaching profession than exist today. Teachers maintain that they are underpaid, and many are; parents justifiably complain that too few teachers are adequately qualified; the government pleads that there is no money for essential materials; children are more difficult to control; reformers believe that the words 'discipline' and 'punishment' should be deleted from dictionaries; and increasing numbers of parents abdicate their responsibility. Some regions are better than others, some schools are fully staffed, but very many have far too few teachers and too many pupils. While a high level of truancy enables some head-teachers and their staff to cope, that still leaves many thousands of children dependent on private tuition. This thriving industry continues to make a major contribution to the number of children producing better-than-average results. Typical examples (from 1985-6 statistics) show that at a school in south London where few, if any, children have private coaching, the average number of 'O' Levels achieved was *one*. In Hertfordshire, at a comprehensive school where eight out of ten pupils had some private tuition, the average number of 'O' Levels jumped to five.

Top-level coaching

This chapter is not really about the merits and demerits of our present educational system. It is simply to highlight the opportunities that exist throughout the country for those offering top-level coaching. Few readers will be able to provide direct training but that should not prevent them from setting up an agency to provide a panel of well-qualified tutors to help children with learning problems.

Another business to start with £100

The money needed to start such an agency is in the region of £150-250. This should cover stationery, postage and local advertising for a few weeks, long enough to get your first clients.

Check out the details

To begin with, telephone your local education authority and check the number of schools in the district and the approximate the number of fifth- and sixth-year schoolchildren studying at any one time. You do not have to mention why you want the information. It is freely available. The figures vary from district to district, and as you will need at least fifty clients to make your business pay, there should be 400-500 students in those categories. Of course, you could always run the business part-time, with your wife or husband filling in the time when you are otherwise occupied. It has excellent possibilities as a second business. Now for the system.

1. You must have printed letter paper. You might call your service 'Hinchfield Tuition Agency', 'Professional Tutors', or some similar title.

Check the competition

2. Having satisfied yourself that there is scope for your business, check Yellow Pages to see if there's any competition in the locality. If so, write, on private stationery, to enquire the details of the services required. It is always worthwhile to be aware of your competition.

Write to head-teachers

3. Write to head-teachers of your local schools on the following lines:

Dear Mr/Mrs/Miss Cosgrove,
The demand for private tuition in this district has prompted me to establish a Tuition Agency. It occurs to me that a number of members of your staff might be interested in providing private tuition to GCSE and 'A' Level students.

Good qualifications essential

All applicants will be expected to have degrees in their own subjects, with a minimum of five years' experience with students studying for these examinations
Completion of confidential application forms will be required, and excellent rates of pay will be paid. If you feel that any members of your staff would be interested, I would be very pleased to hear from you.
Yours sincerely,

(Full name)

4. At the same time, place an advertisement in your local newspaper. The following copy might be considered suitable:

Try an advertisement

HINCHFIELD TUITION AGENCY
would be pleased to hear from well-qualified teachers
interested in giving private tuition
to secondary-level students. Degree essential with
minimum of 5 years' teaching experience at these levels.

Draft your own application form

5. Your application form should be prepared with the name, address and telephone number of your agency on the top. It might read as follows:
Name:
Address and telephone number:
Date of birth:
Degree and where obtained:
History of teaching career to date:
(Allow several lines)
If a language degree, did you spend part of your course in the country concerned?
Which subjects do you prefer to teach?
How many years have you taught these subjects at GCSE standard? 'A' Level standard?
Do you prefer to teach:
a) Boys or girls?
b) GCSE or 'A' Level students?
Which times are most convenient for you to attend for an interview?
Which evenings or days are most convenient for you to teach?
Can you please provide two references indicating the time that you have known each referee.

Signature   Date

Create a news item

6. At the same time, write to the editor of your local newspaper. He should be interested to learn that a professional tuition service has been set up in the area covered by his paper. You might write on the following lines:

Dear Mr Gates,

You may be interested to learn that the above agency has been established to provide a highly qualified tuition service to local students studying for GCSE and 'A' Levels. All our tutors will have degrees and a minimum of five years' experience in teaching at the required level. It is intended that, wherever possible, GCSE students will achieve far better results than average. Students studying for 'A' Levels will be prepared to reach the standards required by universities.

The fees charged will reflect the experience and the high qualifications of all our tutors. Should you require further information I shall be pleased to provide it.

Yours, *etc.* ....

Finding students

7. The only problem now is to find your students. Apart from letting everybody *you* can think of know, place suitably worded cards in windows and take space in your local paper for classified advertising.

It is fair to say that only people with a reasonable standard of education should attempt to start this business. Your tutors should be paid direct and they should be responsible to you for 20 per cent of their fees. It will be hard work getting this business launched, but there should be no shortage of pupils. Many parents are very conscious of the competition which will face their children when they leave school. It is worth mentioning that many immigrant families are particularly interested in private tuition for their children. And, of course, the good results achieved by your tutors almost guarantees recommendations.

Extra free publicity

If you have a very high percentage of success, do let the editor of your local newspaper know. He will be pleased to hear of local success, and it's good publicity for you.

Finally, do not set out to offer a cheap service. Your customers are investing in short-term achievement. If you are confident in your tutors, never charge less than the going rate.

Commission Agencies

The businesses outlined in this section are directly related to established businesses which offer excellent opportunities for self-employment as an agency. Apart from independence, they frequently provide substantial on-going profits.

Though demanding initiative and hard work, they do not require the same disciplines as those businesses dealt with in previous chapters.

27

ADVERTISING

Appeal to the few

This chapter is likely to appeal to only a minority of readers: at first glance, the idea of any inexperienced, unknowledgeable person entering this highly professional and competitive world, is bordering on the ridiculous. But then, the advertising business covers a vast area, and most of us never stop to think of its scope and its ramifications.

Real income possibilities

This chapter is only going to deal with one tiny side of this large, influential profession — the side where those with fairly limited qualifications can earn substantial incomes. This is the area where opportunities are provided by local newspapers. They, like the national press, are dependent on their display advertisers for most of their profits. Starting an 'Agency for Advertising in the Local Media' is not easy, but it is far less difficult than most people imagine. Before going into it in detail anyone contemplating such a venture should be satisfied that they meet *all* the following criteria:

Formal wear

1. That you like wearing a suit and a collar and tie. This is not a business for people who lounge around in T-shirts, jeans and sandals. That sort of gear is sometimes acceptable in the high-flyers in the big agencies, but in the small, local networks, the customers tend to be more conservative. Many of them still like their advisers to look like business people and not as if they are survivors from a disco colony.
2. That you like meeting people because you get on well with them.
3. That you have the patience, the stamina and sufficient means to start a business which is not only demanding but is unlikely to produce any income for a month or two.
4. That the thought does not worry you that you will only get business from a small percentage of the people on whom you call.

5. That you are prepared to read innumerable pages of newspaper advertising in order to be able to talk intelligent shop to your potential customers.

If this doesn't sound like you at all, move on to the next chapter. This one is probably for just a few people who, even at this stage, quite like the idea.

To get started

To get started you need to establish an agency with a local newspaper. They are all desperate for more advertisers, and on the basis that you are only being paid a commission on results, you should not have too much difficulty in being accepted. It is important, however, that *you* should be considered a competent agent and not an odd-job salesman. So before you set foot near the newspaper offices, get hold of at least the last twenty issues of their paper and read them thoroughly. Then carry out the following exercises:

Getting prepared

* Measure the total number of advertising columns per issue.
* Ascertain the cost per column and then calculate the approximate advertising income which the paper produces.

Worthwhile homework

* Count up the number of advertisers and put them into columns according to the size of their advertisements.
Then, on a separate sheet of paper draw up a table of the advertisers, their businesses, and the number of column inches taken by each of their ads. The record will look like this:

| ADVERTISER | BUSINESS | Column inches | | |
		Up to 10	10-20	Over 20
Longwells	Supermarket		X	
Biffin	Furniture		X	
Barkers	Restaurant	X		
Toyota	Cars			X

Train your memory

Take your time and study the records which you have made for each issue and then check how many advertisers have taken space regularly. Now comes an important and slightly more difficult task. Put your papers aside and try to memorise what you have written, particularly the names. Keep doing this until you have a very clear idea of the advertising content of the paper with which you hope to do business. Finally, revert back to the copies of the newspaper and check the number of classified advertisement columns carried and the headings with the longest and the shortest lists. At this point you should know enough about the kind of advertising carried by this particular paper to give you the confidence to contact the advertising manager.

Nerves under control

This is a crunch time. The moment when knees feel a little weak, mouths get dry and hands become clammy. The main reason why people suffer such reactions is that they do not plan their approach carefully. Those who do, quickly overcome their nervousness.

Just pick up the telephone

Unlike many other situations, when an introductory letter might be written, this is one where you should pick up the telephone and speak to the individual concerned. But that is what you do the second time you phone. The first time, you simply ask the telephonist for the name of the advertising manager. If she is bright enough to ask why you want it, explain that you are an advertising agency.

Armed with the intelligence you have gathered and the name of the person who can put you in business, all you need to do at this stage is rehearse your telephone call. Remember, this individual is the advertising manager of a local newspaper, he or she is not managing the Press Association. Your approach should be made in such a way that the person on the other end of the line should be eager to see you. Until you become accustomed to making such calls or attending the meetings that follow, you must prepare and rehearse your conversations.

Rehearse your lines

Write out exactly how you are proposing to open the conversation and, if necessary, how you are going to keep it going. Many people gain confidence rehearsing in front of a mirror. In any event, the conversation should be kept as short as possible and go along the following lines:

No long introduction

'Good morning, Mr Jason. My name is Ascot of the Ascot Advertising Agency.'
'Yes, Mr Ascot.'
Some people find this three-word response quite off-putting. All too often the words do not have a friendly ring about them and the caller feels he is intruding on someone's precious time. You will not be perturbed at all because you will have rehearsed precisely what you

are going to say. You will not hesitate or cough or 'hmm' or do anything other than answer immediately in a controlled, confident voice. 'I would like to discuss placing a large volume of advertising with your newspaper.'

Words that press the greed button

In one short line you will have pressed Mr Jason's greed button to a point where your words are music to him. You are no longer the caller interrupting his thinking or his meeting, you are potential business. All Mr Jason can hear are the words 'large volume of advertising' ringing in his ears. He will be impatient to fix an early meeting but that will not suit you. You are now making the running and the earliest time you can see Mr Jason is at least a week away. You will need all that time to prepare yourself. The next week is hard work.

Holding your advantage

You will be spending every available hour carrying out your own market research. This is a major investment and should take the following form:

Your own research

* Walking down as many streets as time permits, you will make a note of all the major shops, showrooms, garages and suppliers who have not advertised in the newspaper recently. Later you will memorise as many as you can in case you need to drop the odd name when you meet Mr Jason.
* When you recognise the name of a shop-keeper who does advertise, wait until he is not busy and then call on him. Tell him that you are conducting market research and ask him:

Learn the questions and listen to the answers

1. Is he a satisfied advertiser?
2. Does he believe it brings him more business?
3. Does he believe it helps him keep his customers?
4. Does he consider the cost reasonable?
5. Does he actually read the newspaper himself?

Twenty or so records like that will prove invaluable when you are endeavouring to sell space to non-advertisers.

You are now ready to rehearse your meeting with Mr Jason. You have more than sufficient facts to give you all the confidence you need. You will be able to answer without hesitation and with honesty because you will be prepared. You can anticipate that the meeting will go something like this, bearing in mind that Mr Jason is already looking forward to hearing about the business that you are going to introduce.

Your first meeting

Jason: 'What type of business do you think you can introduce, Mr Ascot?'
You (Smile and take your time): 'Well, my agency has carried out a fair amount of research, and I am quite convinced that many traders in this town could be persuaded to become regular advertisers. After all' — *speak slowly and knowledgeably* — 'if you take the High Street alone, eighty-five per cent of the shops down there haven't taken space in your paper for the last three months.'

Impress with facts

At this point throw out one of your hands for effect. 'A big store like Longwells, for instance ... they never seem to take more than a quarter of a page at a time.'
If you are given the chance to continue, carry on. 'I have no doubt that I could bring you advertisements; after all, in an average week you are carrying about Y advertisements taking up around Z columns — that's from a town with more than X number of businesses.' *(You can obtain this last figure from the local Chamber of Commerce.)*

Talk figures

Then add casually, 'I can't believe it would be that difficult to bring in another £10,000 of billings a month.' This is the point where you should give him a chance to say something. If you have to stop earlier, make sure you get the last line in somewhere. The rough figure you quote is related to the income you hope it will produce for you to make it worth your while.
Now be prepared for two situations. The first is when Mr Jason asks you how long you have been in the business. Answer truthfully, 'I haven't been in this business very long but I have spent a great deal of time studying your newspaper and its advertising content.' Whatever you do, do not refer to being made redundant or being out of work.

Be bold

Remember, you are planning to negotiate a contract, you are not looking for sympathy. Furthermore, you are not unemployed, you are starting a business.

Watch the contract

The second point to watch is the commission agreement. Mr Jason's job is to make profits for his newspaper. He may well not be too sensitive about taking advantage of an innocent beginner. He might offer you between 10 and 12 per cent on new advertisements you secure for him once they have been paid for. This is the catch.

Insist on your own terms

Boldly but politely, you tell Mr Jason that his offer is unacceptable. Your terms are 10 or 12 per cent on every advertisement which is placed as a result of your introduction. In this way, if a client advertises every month, you receive commission every month. Instead of one-off commissions you will be building up a business with a renewal income. Both you and he know that advertising revenue is the life-blood of his newspaper. If your terms are refused, do not argue.

Calling bluff

Stand up, smile, hold out your hand to Mr Jason and tell him you are sorry that you cannot do business with him. Unless he is quite the wrong man for his job he will not let you go. Regardless of the expression on his face, your talk of another £10,000 income a month is the best news he's heard for a long time. When he agrees to an on-going commission arrangement, express your pleasure and ask for the terms in writing.

Solicitor time

When you receive the letter, have it checked by a solicitor. It will cost you far less than having to retain him later on to fight a case for you because you didn't understand the agreement.

Once this is settled, you are almost ready to start your new life in the advertising business.

Add to know-how

Although not essential, it could pay dividends for you to spend a day or two with the newspaper staff concerned with the actual laying-out of the advertisements. It would enable you to appreciate the work involved, the composition of the paper itself, and the form each advertisement takes. This will not make you an authority on newspapers or on advertising, but it will give you a little better idea of what the business is all about. It also means that you will be able to tell your potential clients about it if you think they're interested.

Use your bank manager

The time has now arrived when you should visit your bank manager and tell him exactly what you propose to do. Apart from any advice concerning a new account in the name of your business, he will be able to recommend you an accountant, whom you can contact when you are ready. In the meantime, order some printed paper with the name of your new firm, and reckon that you are now in the advertising media business.

The first steps

You have reached the stage when you have to decide which traders to approach first and exactly what line you are going to adopt. There are no golden rules, for you are sure to have some disappointments and some bad experiences wherever you begin. This is nothing to do with the advertising business, it is the fire which every salesman has to go through before he establishes himself. It will be tough going, with numerous frustrations, but if you can keep your cool, every call you make, every conversation you have, will teach you something. You might start by calling on a competitor of a tradesman who has advertised a few times recently.

Prepare your lines

This man will already be well aware of the local paper and the fact that people advertise in it. Instead of opening with words about the paper, your approach should be more positive and arresting. You are going to walk into this shop smiling and determined not to rush your words. After the usual greeting, come straight out with 'My firm has just completed an extensive research project which I believe affects your business.' Wait for a reaction but if it is not forthcoming, simply carry on: 'We are convinced that you could substantially increase your trade.' (Note that you are now switching to 'we' as you are speaking on behalf of your firm.)

Hold your advantage

However cynical a trader is, he is going to listen to anything that might improve his profits. At that moment you have his attention and it is important that you keep it by retaining his interest.

Good bait

'What we have discovered', you say, 'is how one of your competitors continues to get new customers every month.' If possible, don't let him interrupt, but go straight on to say, 'He decided that he could only

THE A-Z OF SELF EMPLOYMENT

expand by investing a certain percentage of his overheads in continually building up his business.' Stop there for the inevitable question.

When it comes, you answer, 'You have a competitor in this town who regularly advertises in the *XK Gazette*. The only reason he does it is because it pays him handsomely to do so.'

Moment of truth

Hesitate for a second. 'Our research shows that it could do the same for you.' This is the moment of truth. Either he will dismiss you or he will accept your suggestion that you work out an advertising programme for him to help him measure the possible benefits for his business.

Free service

This is a service which you are offering free without obligation. If it works, pass the enquiry back to Mr Jason in writing and ask him to prepare a quotation for you.

Time for courtesy

It's probably going to take a little while, so, on your new headed paper, write to your potential customer, thank him for the courtesy he afforded you and undertake to make a 'presentation' to him very shortly.

That is one approach. If it doesn't produce positive results immediately, do not judge it until you have tried it a reasonable number of times. In any event, keep a record of every meeting, noting the reception you receive, the position and age of the person you spoke to and your feelings about the particular business.

Solo space offer

You might also consider calling on those who do not advertise but whose competitors are also not advertising. In such cases you will be in a position to offer them a 'solo' position offer in the paper. An opportunity to be the only firm in their business whose advertisement will be placed in the paper for a given period. You would have to clear this with Mr Jason, but he should be delighted because it's business which he isn't getting now and isn't likely to get in the normal course of events.

Analyse your daily progress

At the end of each day, go over every call you made. Try to recognise the reasons why you were well received by some people and not by others. You might try to recall the attention which each person gave you when you were speaking to them. Did you think they were anti-advertising? Too worried about their overheads to risk spending any more? Too smug about their business? Unimpressed with your story-line? Too distracted to give you the necessary attention? Or was it possibly the wrong day for them to talk about advertising? Always note whether you think it worthwhile to call again, and when. A parting remark might be a special offer to keep space for the trader to announce his next sale. It might just keep the door open.

Very soon you will begin to develop your own selling style. You will realise that you are helping people to build up or maintain their share of local trade. Using your imagination to interest new clients makes you an entrepreneur not a gimmick merchant. The former builds businesses, the latter will only build a bad reputation.

A great attraction of this business is continuity. Every time one of your introductions places an advertisement, you will earn commission. It follows that, if you are able continually to bring in new clients, your income must increase as your old clients go on placing advertisements. There comes a point, if all goes well, when your business is self-generating. Another big up-side is the different people you meet. Many will have time for a chat, and from them you will get new ideas and possibly introductions too. If, at the end of the day, you should decide that advertising is not for you, you will be much better placed to consider the opportunities for some other type of enterprise.

A good business

Whatever happens, always appear cheerful and optimistic. So long as you are in this business it is because you believe it is a good business, even if it is going through a slow period.

28

FLORIST SERVICES

Read this carefully

Let nobody be in any doubt, operating a florist business is only for the experienced. It is not enough to have capital, or even flair and an artistic temperament. Without experience, failure is almost inevitable. Even with it, such an enterprise can be precarious. But, like many businesses, there is one side of it that continues to prosper if one can get it right.

Knowing the business

Contract work is the most interesting, the most demanding, and certainly the most profitable. Providing fresh flowers and plants to restaurants, offices and showrooms is a highly specialised service; those who are successful in it have made it their business to understand every aspect of it. They are the professionals. They know which flowers are best for each client, how to arrange the blooms or plants, how to look after them, when to renew them, and how to charge for them.

Big money

One quite small firm in the City of London has a turnover well in excess of £500,000 a year. The owner works hard, but in the space of only a few years he has become a very wealthy man.

No flying leap

Considering the demanding nature of this business and the qualifications of those who make a success of it, many readers might be wondering how this chapter made its way into this book. Well they might, because the concept will probably only have a limited appeal. It is not suggested that anyone takes a flying leap into setting up an up-market contract florist — but without any capital investment other than time, and with no knowledge, the opportunity arises in finding new clients for the established flower houses.

For those who find the idea attractive, there is eventually a very good living to be made.

No cash outlay

There is no investment to find, but it is unlikely that you will be paid much, if anything, by the florist until you actually produce business. Before beginning on that road, it is essential that you endeavour to spend at least a week or two in the shops getting to know the type of clientele they attract and what their clients require.

Watch the contract

Then, subject to a satisfactory agreement, you could be ready to go out into a world where many are waiting for you. Let us not, however, dismiss the contract too quickly. Its details are vital. You should have no difficulty in persuading a florist to pay a reasonable commission for an introduction: you can probably expect between 10 and 20 per cent, depending on the size of the order. This, at first sight, is not unreasonable, but it is not sufficient. Your agreement should grant you a high commission for, say one to three months, and then a lower commission for as long as the account is serviced by the florist. It should be treated as your account, and you should ensure that your own solicitor is satisfied with the wording of your letter of agreement. It is important that it should enable you to build your own renewal income.

Family benefit

If you become a success, it could make good sense to operate through a company so that the commissions will continue to accrue to your family even if you meet the proverbial bus.

Anyone who shudders or feels bored at the thought of talking about flowers to restaurateurs, showroom managers, hoteliers and the like, should not give another thought to the idea; indeed, it is probably not particularly interesting to the vast majority of people, who will have already moved on to the next chapter. But the few who are still reading might like to know the following facts:

So many opportunities

* Thousands of restaurants and shops have fresh flowers provided daily. The opportunity for an enthusiastic salesman arises because even more thousands do not.
* Thousands of shops and offices do not have flowers simply because no one has taken the trouble to offer them the service. Most florists are far too worried

about making their business pay to do anything more than send out leaflets to promote new business.

* In the famous salons in London, leading couturiers spend hundreds of pounds every week decorating their showrooms. One firm is estimated to spend £25,000 a year, and there are others who spend even more. There are, of course, very many in every major city in the country who spend between £5,000 and £10,000 a year.

* Funerals and weddings provide excellent one-off business for the florist, but commercial contracts with showrooms and offices often continue for years and are almost inflation-proof.

Goodwill just goes on and on

Of course, many business houses are not going to profess interest, but that is where the art of selling comes in. There is considerable scope for large floral decor in the entrance halls to banks, motor showrooms, clubs, large firms of solicitors, accountants, insurance brokers or architects, and all the offices where major clients are likely to be impressed by extravagant good taste. Such splendid displays usually lead to recommendations.

Sales aid

A very useful tip when you call on potential customers: take a small selection of photographs of large and small arrangements which your firm is capable of undertaking. These could be your greatest sales aids.

For anyone who has little money, loves flowers and enjoys selling, this is still an opportunity with many possibilities. (See also 'Flower Making', page 51.)

29

LIFE INSURANCE

Bad and good news

There are few businesses with a bigger turnover of sales staff than the life insurance industry. One large company recently admitted that they take on less than twenty out of every hundred applicants, and no more than five are still with them at the end of three months. That is the bad news. The good news is that there are several thousand self-employed life insurance salesmen earning well over £20,000 a year, and a good number more than double that figure. The interesting fact is that the vast majority of these successful men and women were previously employed in quite unrelated occupations.

Forget about too much luck

Before anyone runs away with the idea that selling life insurance is an easy business, it is important to emphasise that it is an area where there is frequent sales resistance, enormous professional competition, and far too many part-time pseudo-agents. Some believe, quite wrongly, that it is largely a business in which luck plays a significant part. In reality, as well as having at least some basic knowledge of life insurance, it is important for a potentially successful agent to have the ability to get on well with people, and the determination to work long hours.

This is a constant effort business

This is a business where consistent effort brings its own reward, and time is a commodity to be invested generously, not calculated. Patience is an asset, intelligence a requirement, and enthusiasm an essential.

No capital — but ....

Even though there are many opportunities and no initial capital is required, life insurance will only appeal to a limited number of readers of this book. It is for their benefit that the following guidelines are given.

Know your competition

1. The business falls broadly into three categories:

a) The large professional consultancy, including major firms of life insurance brokers.

b) General insurance brokers, accountants and, unfortunately, almost anyone who can be persuaded by one or other of the life insurance companies or brokers to accept a sub-agency.

c) Agents who only work for one company.

2. Initially, anyone starting in this business would be well advised to seek employment with one major life insurance office specialising in direct sales. Companies like Allied Dunbar, Confederation Life, and other leaders who employ their own independent sales forces are likely to offer the best opportunities.

Good training free

Despite the fact that you must expect to be remunerated almost entirely by commission, you would have the advantage of some initial training, access to considerable advice, and the benefit of working with others who face the same opportunities, challenges and problems as yourself.

Experts always available to help

In addition, competent practitioners with many years of experience will always be readily available to you to meet your clients and help you to complete a transaction. These advantages cannot be exaggerated, particularly as they have often been responsible for the progress of those who made a real success in the business.

3. Accept the fact that even after your first course, your knowledge of the business will be modest. You will be equipped to sell a limited number of contracts to people in given circumstances. That does not mean that your earning potential is automatically limited. Not at all. It simply means that, when in any doubt, you will not hesitate to call in the experts. They are there to help you. They are there to ensure that you will not prejudice your reputation or the reputation of your company by attempting to answer questions when you are uncertain.

Tread gently

4. Pounding the streets for new business is just about the most soul-destroying exercise that anyone can undertake. Relying on relatives and friends to take out policies with you might be helpful in the short term, but is unlikely to help

you build a solid foundation. More often than not, you risk becoming short of friends and estranged from your relatives.

5. Once you have the necessary confidence to go out and sell, time should be taken to consider a specific area on which to concentrate. Some agents will advise you to nag your friends and acquaintances for introductions. Others will suggest that you offer accountants, house agents and garage owners half your commission. These ideas have all been known to work, but only your personal chemistry can tell you if you want to build a business using these methods. If you have well-connected friends, their introductions could, of course, be invaluable. If not, you will only be making a nuisance of yourself by approaching them for favours which they cannot grant. Accountants and house agents are in a position to introduce business, and sometimes, if one is fortunate, one can rely on continuous support from them. More often than not, they either have their own agencies or existing arrangements with brokers who, in turn, introduce business to them.

Worth giving half commission

Never place too much reliance on loyalty when making sub-agency arrangements. Furthermore, such people tend to be greedy and you will be lucky if you are left with 50 per cent of the commission you earn. It could rightly be argued that it is business which you would otherwise not obtain but, equally, you have to get twice as much of it to make it worth while. In the beginning one has to try every avenue to find business but, taking the longer view, personal sales planning is more certain to pay sizeable dividends.

Following US methods that have produced vast incomes

6. Compared to the American salesmen, the English are novices. It is true that the average American and his wife are much keener on life assurance, but then his agent sells much harder. It is a quite common practice for an American to ask his potential son-in-law to disclose the amount of life cover which he is carrying or proposing to effect. When an American executive receives an increase in salary, he automatically raises his life insurance cover. It has become a status symbol like a golf handicap, a chest measurement or a more expensive swimming-pool. That is a country where business men work hard enough to support a disproportionately high number of heart specialists and psychiatrists, and where there are more wealthy widows than anywhere else on earth.

Once in a while is still worthwhile

It is therefore not surprising that there are a good number of American insurance journals published every month. Most of them are unbelievably full of pathetic waffle and stories of successful gimmick-selling exploits. However, every once in a while these magazines produce an idea, an article or a story the significance of which can be profitably applied by life assurance salesmen in England.

If you only get one good idea a year, it can pay for your magazine subscriptions and even your holidays for the rest of your life. More often than not, such ideas are not remotely sophisticated and it is frequently their simplicity that makes them attractive and easy to sell.

Simple and profitable

The following are two examples of selling techniques which worked very profitably for two very different salesmen in the States.

Who was Edward A. Wexler?

Edward A. Wexler was a man who built his business exploiting emotions. He cultivated the voice and the facial expressions to meet his aspirations. He convinced himself that he was a kind, sympathetic, sensitive, sincere man who was created to serve others. He built an extremely successful business by playing on the emotions of his clients. One day, in 1960, he endeavoured to sell a $250,000 life policy to Bill Schultz, the owner of the local radio station.

Short of $2,000

Bill genuinely wanted to buy that large policy, if only to boast about it at the golf club, but he simply lacked the first $2,000 premium. Ed took his time relating real and imaginary stories about young fathers who were unable to pass medical examinations by the time they were thirty-six, and of others who dropped dead or were run over, leaving their gorgeous kids dependent on mean relatives and indifferent friends.

A real deal

When he was certain that Bill was thoroughly miserable, Wexler offered him a deal: he would advance the first annual premium if, in return, Bill agreed to allow him to make the first announcement on the local radio programme every day for ten years. Bill liked the concept, but knocked the time span down to five years. The policy was effected. Ed paid the $2,000 and received $1,200 back in commission. Then, every day, at 6.30 a.m. a recording of his voice could be heard by thousands of families and fathers driving to work uttering a variety of messages like:

Corny maybe, but very effective

'Good morning, this is Edward A. Wexler calling to wish every kid in this county the best of luck today. I simply adore kids so much I have made it my business to look after them. All I do is design life insurance policies specially for mums and dads who really love their kids. If you are one of those wonderful parents, why not telephone me, on my private line, Central ——, and have a chat.'

Edward Wexler sold more life insurance than any other salesman in that entire state. Five years later, he was happy to pay Bill Schultz $20,000 a year for a new contract. It is less than likely that he would have been a big hit in a small town in England, but this true story does illustrate the American attitude to life insurance.

The second salesman, John Pensky, built a successful agency without playing on people's emotions. While all his competitors would be quoting premiums of say, £1,000, $1,080, $1,150, for a given life policy, with the same sum assured but with different frills, John had developed his own line. He never referred to the actual premium. He would ask the client how much he was paying for his overdraft — in those days the rate was about 6 per cent.

The 2 per cent interest line

'That's interesting, six per cent eh?' John would begin quietly. 'Do you realise that for less than two per cent an institution with as much muscle as the Bank of America would guarantee your family $100,000 if anything happened to you? That money would be deposited in the name of your family just in case you were one of the X hundred thousand unlucky guys who didn't make the end of this year or any other year.'

John Pensky claimed that this was the winning approach that made him life insurance salesman of every year for years for his entire company.

It also worked in England

The English life insurance broker who read about Pensky's success applied the same principle in the UK, and was also highly successful. Subsequently, he claimed to have sold millions of pounds of life assurance from following the less corny examples which he gleaned from American magazines.

It is not suggested that the above examples would achieve the same results today. But the method applied to successful selling is just as important as finding the client.

Young women are good clients

One relatively untapped field is the young highly paid secretary, still living at home with her parents. Financially, she is in clover. She is more interested in music, boys, holidays and her car than she is in life insurance. In fact, she isn't interested in life insurance. But, with few exceptions, she is interested in getting married eventually, or at least in having her own flat or house. This then is the key. To offer a policy which would:

Help them plan a home

1. Make it easier for her to get a mortgage when she wanted it.
2. Make it cheaper in the long term.
3. Reduce the term of the mortgage when she eventually requires it.
4. Give her a substantial profit earlier than could be expected because she is planning her house purchase before she actually needs it.

All this can be achieved because a with-profit endowment policy can be used to repay a mortgage, and the sooner the policy is effected, the sooner it will mature.

Sell the end product

To be successful, it is necessary to attach an 'end product' to the policy you are selling. Simply to tell a father that your policy would guarantee £5,000 for his newborn son when the child reaches the age of twenty-one, is not very original. Why not suggest that the proud father could give his son a 'special holiday' or his first car or twenty racks of fine wine?

The Americans are right in one respect: life insurance is sold, it is not often bought. With so many enjoying company benefits and pension schemes, more time needs to be spent in preparing tailor-made recommendations for each client. A company like Allied Dunbar offers a number of very attractive, financial products for an agent with the right qualities and determination to succeed.

A very good business for women

Although mostly identified with men, life insurance is also an ideal business for women. Not sufficient numbers appreciate that they have all the right qualities to make them enormously successful in this highly profitable business. Yet, many women have just the right understanding, intuition, intelligence, personality and approach to make them ideally suited to accept the challenge and make a great success of it. More women should realise that life insurance almost invariably concerns family life, mothers and children — so surely it is an ideal field in which women can play a very active part?

You must believe in it

Words of warning: life insurance has a great deal to offer as a business but it is no good for anyone who is half-hearted about it. Only those who believe in themselves, in the insurance concept, and in the contracts they will be selling, should even entertain the idea. Speak to one or two direct-selling companies and some of their top salesmen before committing yourself. If you feel it right for you, it could be interesting, stimulating and profitable. If not, it will not be a disaster, as you will not have invested any capital, but it will be a disappointment. Think about it carefully.

Contact the right people

If you decide it is the right business for you, contact the Life Insurance Association. This organisation, which is entirely concerned with serving life insurance brokers and agents, can offer excellent advice and, in addition, it has negotiated a very comprehensive and competitive policy for those who require professional indemnity protection.

Miscellaneous

THE IMPORTANT SECTION
WHICH SHOULD BE READ
BY EVERYONE SERIOUSLY
THINKING ABOUT
STARTING A BUSINESS.

30

A SIGNIFICANT LIST

The following names have been cited in the press as among the most progressive companies in Britain, described as far-sighted and very concerned with helping people on to their feet. This is certainly not a complete list — over 100,000 companies have said that they want to be included in this category.

This list is referred to a number of times in this book and, wherever possible, you should make use of it; the details of the companies are readily available from The Manpower Services Commission, Norfolk Chamber, 11 Norfolk Row, Sheffield. For the purpose of this book, the following serves as a useful reference to illustrate the possibilities for those wishing to contact major companies who might use their services or products.

MARKS & SPENCER PLC
J. SAINSBURY PLC
THE BURTON GROUP
ALLIED-LYONS PLC
THE BOOTS COMPANY PLC
CADBURY-SCHWEPPES PLC
NORTHERN FOODS PLC
TESCO STORES PLC
SHELL UK
GEC PLC
RANK XEROX
ICI PLC
IBM UK LIMITED
IMPERIAL GROUP PLC
UNILEVER UK
EAGLE STAR INSURANCE

WHITBREAD & COMPANY PLC
THE DISTILLERS COMPANY
ESSO UK PLC
TARMAC PLC
ASDA-MFI GROUP PLC
THE POST OFFICE
THE PLESSEY CO PLC
GLAXO HOLDINGS
ROLLS-ROYCE LIMITED
THORN EMI
GEORGE WIMPEY PLC
JOHN LEWIS PLC
COURTAULDS PLC
LITTLEWOODS
THE BOC GROUP

When you think any of the firms mentioned could be useful, simply look them up in the telephone directory. Phone and ask for the name of the chairman and start your letter to him as follows:

Dear Mr X,
Your company is well known among those concerned with helping and training the unemployed. However, I am not looking for training or for a job but I would very much appreciate your....

You will find that, particularly as you are not seeking employment or a loan, the majority of people will be happy to be helpful.

31

FOR
WOMEN
PARTICULARLY

It is invariably a mistake to generalise. Nearly every business referred to in this book can be launched and operated equally successfully by women as by men. But there are some which, on balance, can best be undertaken by women. This is not necessarily a matter of ability but, more often than not, one of temperament, experience or chemistry. Furthermore, certain occupations are more identified with women than with men. There are men who knit and sew and look after children as well as many women, but they tend to be the exceptions.

In practical terms, a number of businesses in this section are ideally suited to be undertaken by a wife-husband team, as will no doubt become apparent as specific projects are considered. There are a few hints which are worth giving at this stage. They apply just as much to men as to women. The reason for mentioning them here is because women are often more prone to pursue an exercise on impulse. Alternatively, like many men, they wonder where their thinking should begin. For the benefit of those who may have opened the book at this chapter, the following questions should be answered before seriously entertaining any business:

1. Are you starting this business for fun, for pocket money, to cover essential overheads, for holidays, or in order to produce an income on which you can live?
2. Are you going to enjoy doing it? Are you going to get some satisfaction as well as money from it? Or, deep down, do you fear you could get bored out of your mind or aggravated beyond your coping abilities?

3. If you are proposing to work at home, do think about other members of the family. Are they going to be supportive or is your little business going to be the cause of constant bickering?

Above all else, remember that women are just as capable of starting a business as are men. Furthermore, the majority have an added advantage — they have feminine charm, with which few men can compete.

32

LUCK: THE FAILURE'S DESCRIPTION OF SUCCESS

SOME CASE HISTORIES

The majority of fortunate people have created their own luck. Of course, the son of a wealthy father starts life with a built-in advantage. But if he misuses it, the long-term benefits are minimal. When considering luck in the context of this book, it is best to ignore it. Some people have hit the jackpot by chance or discovered gold in their back garden, but only a fool would plan his future on such remote possibilities. Even worse are those who convince themselves that others who make it in life have only luck to thank. It is so rarely the case, one is well advised to forget it.

Regardless of this, luck is a word so often used in relation to the successful achievements of men and women that it is worth devoting a few paragraphs to considering it in a little more detail. Probably the best way to illustrate luck is to consider the careers of three men described as 'lucky'.

When A.J. (Fred) Archer, an underwriter at Lloyd's, consistently made exceptionally good profits, a less successful colleague was overheard to say, 'That chap was born lucky.' The truth was that Fred was one of a large family dogged by misfortune. His parents had died when he was six years old, and he had spent his boyhood in an orphanage. He emerged at the age of sixteen, penniless, without any plan of what he was going to do with his life. All he knew was that he was going to work hard and make a determined effort to reach the top somehow, somewhere. It was pure chance that he applied for, and was offered, a job as an office boy in the very conservative world of Lloyd's of London; this mecca of international insurance tended to employ young men from 'good' families or with well-recognised connections. To Fred, Lloyd's was the home of opportunity, but it could just as soon have been Barclays Bank, Marks & Spencer or any other business house. He worked hard and conscientiously and earned the very modest wages that were paid in pre-war days. In addition, he made it his business to listen, to ask questions, to make a mental note of answers, and to show a keen interest in the role of his seniors. Within a few years he was permitted to spend some time sitting near the underwriters who actually accepted insurance risks. Watching, listening and questioning, he began to have ideas of his own. It was not a fast process, but, in the course of time, Fred, the reliable young man from the orphanage, was considered to have talent. When the opportunity came to play a more active part in underwriting, he grabbed it. He applied all the knowledge he had gained over the years and stuck rigidly to a well-thought-out underwriting policy. It paid off and continued to pay off, and Fred became a highly respected successful underwriter. Those who did not know his background continued to call him lucky.

A young man named John Cohen had little money but considerable ambition. He managed to borrow a small sum, and started to buy and sell tins of food. Unlike his competitors, he made very little profit on each tin. But his reputation for being cheap soon spread, and he was soon selling far more tins than anyone else in the business in that area. When someone suggested that he should open a shop, it made good sense to him. When he worked out the additional overheads, however, he realised that even a small shop would take at least half of his profits. So, instead, he bought an old lorry, stacked up his tins, and sold them off the tail-board. Careful thinking and even more careful planning became the hallmark of the man who founded Tesco, the great supermarket chain. He retained his cockney accent and developed no airs. He became well-known as a shrewd, honest trader whose motto was 'Pile it high and sell it cheap', and well-loved as a generous multi-millionaire. When John Cohen received his much deserved knighthood, there were those who declared, 'He's always been lucky'.

Charley Cosgrove was born with a weak chest in a damp council flat. His poor health prevented him from indulging in sport, and having to share his small bedroom with a young brother made studying very difficult. Nonetheless, he worked hard. When his brother spent hours kicking a ball round the back yard or watching TV, Charley would spend the time reading his books. Eventually, he passed both 'O' Levels and 'A' Levels, and the time came to consider the right job for him. To the amazement of his parents, Charley obtained a grant sufficient to enable him to study medicine, if he could manage to live on a pittance. Away from home with a room of his own, he found no difficulty in concentrating on his studies. He excelled. At the end of the first year he sailed through the examinations with marks which were a record in his medical school.

But, a few months later, Charley's father was killed by a hit-and-run driver, leaving a widow and three children. There was little insurance and no savings, and Charley had to give up his medical studies to help his mother. He could not consider a job that was physically strenuous or one that required him to work in the open air. In any case, the town was full of fit, trained, unemployed men desperate for work, and large numbers of them, applying for every vacancy, discouraged Charley from even joining the queues. His mother found work in the local laundry, and his brother enlisted in the Merchant Navy; for his part, when it wasn't raining, Charley would walk round the streets trying to recognise an opportunity. Near his home was an old hall which had not been used since the new school had been built a few years earlier. Charley discovered that he could rent it for a few pounds a night if he would clean it up with a coat of paint first. With two helpful friends and no experience, the hall was painted. Waiting for the paint to dry, he began searching through all the papers and window notices for anyone who wanted to rent a hall. By the end of the week, Charley had rented the property and had let it to a small pop group. He was in business. This transaction was to be the beginning of the Cosgrove Property Company. Fifteen years of walking the streets, renting and letting unused buildings and, later, buying and selling small shops, made Charley a rich man. When he had secured his mother's financial future and had helped his sister to buy a house, he got married himself. At the reception he was amused to hear himself described as the man born to be lucky.

Perhaps it is worth listing some of the essential ingredients that have contributed to the 'luck' of successful people over the years.
1. Hard work. Believe the tycoon who described his success as 95 per cent perspiration and 5 per cent inspiration.
2. Timing. More ice cream is sold on hot days, and more umbrellas when it's raining. The importance of recognising the right time to buy and to sell cannot be exaggerated.
3. Perseverance. Those who are convinced they are right carefully check what they're doing but they never give up easily.
4. Competition. Never cut your prices at the expense of quality and service. Keep watching presentation and overheads.
5. Imagination. This is often just a question of keeping your eyes open wide enough to recognise an opportunity.
6. Luck. Usually found by men who work for it, rarely by those who only look for it.

The following people all made use of some or all of these ingredients.

The Pitel brothers

Vic Pitel worked in a shipyard for six years. His prime job was unloading, loading and moving timber. It was his responsibility to ensure that every safety precaution was taken in stacking long planks of timber fifteen foot high. He became familiar with examining tarpaulin, ropes, ladders, trolleys, and ground surfaces. It was to his credit that throughout the years when he was in charge of his team, there was not a single accident. Unfortunately, this remarkable record did not prevent him from being made redundant when the shipping slump hit his employers.

Rajid Pitel, a year younger than his brother, was employed on an industrial building-site. He drove a motorised trolley to bring the materials to the carpenters and to the slate- and brick-layers. It was left to him to remove cracked tiles and broken bricks and draw the foreman's attention to any wooden planks which were not perfect. The pay with overtime gave Rajid a very satisfactory income. When the company was made bankrupt, he joined the ranks of the unemployed. Having applied unsuccessfully for many vacancies, he feared that he could be without a job indefinitely.

After a few months without even a part-time job, Vic took stock of his assets. He owned a seven-year-old car worth £250, and had about £300 left in the Post Office. Without knowing how to begin, he decided that he was going to start his own business. All he needed was an idea. He spent several weeks walking round shopping parades similar to the one described in Chapter 1, but he failed to feel remotely encouraged. It became increasingly apparent that he lacked the training for every business that occurred to him. Gradually, he became disillusioned and started to think his misfortune was the fault of his parents, his poor education, his financial position, and colour prejudice. Vic Pitel began to stay in bed later each morning, he frequently forgot to shave, and often allowed his growing depression to increase his impatience. But he was still not prepared to stand around on street corners advertising his despondency.

One day, he arrived at a shopping parade at 11.30. As had become his practice, he walked from one shop to another in the hope that something would register. Nothing did until he saw a window-cleaner washing the windows of a clothing store which had a frontage of forty feet. The following three things registered in Vic's mind:

1. The number of people who deliberately avoided the shop.
2. That the window cleaner's ladder was too short.
3. The ladder looked insecure.

Vic rushed home, shaved, changed into his best jeans and a clean shirt, and walked back to the shopping precinct. On the way, he rehearsed exactly what he was going to say to the shopkeeper.

Confidently, he told the man that he was sure the shop was losing substantial potential trade by having its windows cleaned at such a busy time of the day. He also pointed out that the ladder, too small for the job, without rubber shoes, could easily cause an accident with unpleasant consequences. The shop-keeper was impressed, particularly when Vic offered to clean the windows before the shop opened. His luck was in. He was hired twice a week at the full going rate for the job. On his way back home, he collected Rajid from his favourite street corner and told him they were going to be partners in the window-cleaning business.

The total cash outlay, including the hire of two adjustable ladders for a month, was under £50. Selling the idea of timing and security, it was not long before the brothers were earning as much as their jobs had been paying them.

It was Rajid who came up with the first plan to expand. He had noticed that the frame of one shop was in very poor condition. Neither of them knew how to repair window frames or replace glass but they soon found an established firm that specialised in the field. They negotiated a commission rate of 10 per cent for all business introductions and undertook to do their best to find new customers. This fitted in extremely well with their existing business. They concentrated on window-cleaning early in the day and in the late afternoons, and spent the rest of their time looking for shopfronts in need of repair. This latter enterprise soon added over £200 a week to their earnings. In 1986, this was a substantial increase.

The Pitel brothers extended their business to include repairs, interior decorating and sign-writing. They now employ five staff and own three vans. Both Vic and Rajid own houses which they could never have bought had they stayed in employment.

Roger W. Jenkins

A comfortable father and a reasonably good brain enabled Roger Jenkins to make his way through Harrow to Oxford University. Having obtained a good degree, he spent a year in France polishing up his French and perfecting his skiing. He returned to England to join a public company as a junior executive, confident of his future as the chairman was a family friend. He married at the age of thirty-two, the same year as he was appointed to the main board.

The years that followed were enjoyable, stimulating and profitable. Roger acquired a useful block of shares, enjoyed popularity among his colleagues and frequently confided to his wife, Norma, that he expected to succeed the old chairman one of these days. Subsequently he was shattered to learn that the company was being taken over and that he was to be made redundant. He was fifty.

Roger took the news so badly that he could not bring himself to tell his wife for three months. Eventually, he consulted his doctor. The latter prescribed some mild tranquillisers and convinced him that he simply had to discuss his new position with his wife. That evening, he took his wife out to dinner because he didn't trust himself not to break down if he told her in their home. Norma listened to her husband complaining bitterly about his disappointment, his old chairman and his unrecognised talents. She knew that what he needed was fresh hope, real support and personal encouragement. When he told her about the large number of jobs he had applied for unsuccessfully, she interrupted him.

'Look,' she began, 'This isn't the end of the world. There are countless men who would love to have the chance to start something new at the age of fifty. The fact that it wasn't your choice doesn't mean that it couldn't be a great opportunity. I think you should stop worrying about a job and start thinking about a business.'

For the next few days they did little else but think about the different businesses they could start together. Eventually, it was Norma who came up with a bright idea. Realising that there must be hundreds of middle-aged executives who find themselves redundant, she suggested they should offer an Advisory Service for Top Executives.

They wrote out exactly how they saw the service and the areas of advice which it would cover. Within weeks they had made agreements with the following:

1. Two firms of solicitors prepared to provide legal advice for modest fees.
2. Two firms of chartered accountants prepared to give tax advice for modest fees.
3. Two established firms of insurance brokers, and two firms of pension specialists, who agreed to give their advice free in anticipation of potential business.
4. Two firms of estate agents, who agreed to charge 50 per cent of normal fees where it was decided to recommend clients to release capital by moving to less expensive homes.
5. Two psychologists who might be needed to help cope with special clients.

6. Two banks, who agreed to provide immediate bridging loans with deferred interest for the first three months if necessary.

7. Over a dozen hotels in different parts of the country, who agreed to give discounts up to 20 per cent for those clients who it was felt would benefit from a holiday before accepting a new challenge.

8. A local solicitor to take two small offices in his building with the benefit of switchboard, telex and fax services.

They had good stationery printed, showing the names of all their professional consultants, and drafted several letters, which they were to send out to companies, offering their services to those recently made or about to be made redundant, the idea being that the companies would be prepared to pay the fees.

They arranged meetings with the editors of several newspapers within a radius of twenty miles. All agreed to give publicity to the new firm.

Within two months, Roger and Norma Jenkins had established The Jenkins Advice Centre. They received considerable support from their professional colleagues, who appreciated that the new firm was not in competition. It was a highly specialised business which took off very quickly. Many clients were delighted to find themselves speaking to a man who had been through their own experiences. The Jenkins Advice Centre now has three offices and ten staff.

Andy Turpin

Some young people are not remotely interested in school. Andy Turpin fell into this category. A tall, well-built lad, he was entirely preoccupied with football and girls. When he left school at the age of sixteen, he boasted that he had the best record for playing truant since he was ten years old. His headmaster described him as a boy with untapped ability. He had three jobs in a year, but eventually settled in the spares department of The Hinton Engine Company. His job was to keep hundreds of different items in their own compartments and advise the stores manager when any stocks were running low. In his fourth year he was given the title of Spare Parts Controller with an appropriate rise in wages. Three months later he lost his job when Hintons were taken over.

At this time the streets of South London were full of unemployed young men, many of whom were far better educated than Andy. Apart from the indignity of being unemployed, Andy missed the money. He did not drink or gamble, but he liked the girls and the girls cost money. Without any preconceived ideas he started walking round shopping precincts and factory sites, hoping that he might see an opportunity. He didn't. One day, he met an old girlfriend just entering a supermarket.

In answer to her question, he told her that he was about to start his own business to make real money. The girl was impressed and encouraged Andy to walk round the store with her. She had come to buy a packet of cotton wool balls which she used to take off her make-up. 'It's crazy,' she complained. 'I have to take a large bag to work when I only use three or four a day.'

On the way out Andy noticed outsize rolls of cotton wool and an idea began to emerge. The following day he returned to the supermarket and invested £3 in a roll of cotton wool and a bag of cotton-wool balls. He soon discovered that one roll could produce dozens of bags of balls. Within two weeks, he had produced his own little packs with a difference. Instead of having sixty balls in a bag, he had ten little packs of six cotton-wool balls in a cellophane container. His second investment was to spend £10 having 500 blue labels printed with 'Turpins' Mini-Packs of Cotton-Wool Balls'. At the time that Andy took his first samples to the manager of the supermarket, he had laid out exactly £19.50 in the business he hoped to start. This covered the initial cost of raw materials, a good pair of scissors and a roll of Sellotape. He calculated that if he charged half the price of the existing packs, he would still make a profit of over 100 per cent. To his amazement, the manager took one look at the bag and ordered 500.

Andy promised to deliver within three days and the manager assured him that he would be paid immediately. There was no problem completing the order in time. He used his savings and a small loan from his mother to buy his stock, and two girlfriends helped him fill the bags each evening. When the orders began to roll in, Andy spoke to his father's bank manager who recommended a small firm of accountants to advise him.

Two years later, Andy now markets packs of several different items, including emery boards, safety-pins, face-cleaners and cotton-wool balls. He makes a very good living but still works from his home. He concentrates on buying and finding the orders, with all the packing being carried out by part-time out-workers. He plans to have twenty different packs carrying his name within the next five years.

Sally Holmes

Former schoolteacher and secretary, widow, mother of two young children. When her husband Bob died suddenly at the age of forty-eight, Sally Holmes was faced with a number of alternatives. She could sell her home, move to a small flat, stop the children's music lessons, forget about holidays and try to struggle through on her pension; she could find a job which would still enable her to look after her children; she could remarry, or could try to start a little business.

Her bank manager was convinced that it would be in Sally's interest — and in the long-term interest of the bank — if she remarried; her solicitor needed time to think about the problem, and her accountant recommended her to take a job.

There was no shortage of schoolteachers, particularly of those who hadn't taught for nearly ten years. Sally's secretarial skills were rusty, and most of her applications for jobs remained unanswered. The idea of a small business appealed to her but she was quite convinced that she lacked the ability to buy and sell.

In an effort to recognise her talents, she wrote out the following pen sketch of herself.

Sally Holmes:	42. Short, neat, articulate.
Appearance:	Good — quite attractive, really.
People:	On balance, I like them.
Qualifications:	Teacher. Secretary. Good cook.
Hobbies:	Tennis. Music. Cooking. Reading. Theatre. Children. Writing.
Reading:	Novels. Biographies. Cookery.
Teaching:	No vacancies.
Secretarial	No vacancies.
Nursery School:	Not interested.
Finances:	£3,000 a year short — figure rising.
Friends:	None likely to be helpful.

Sally went off to the local library to see if any of the books might give her an idea. She looked through all the volumes on business, decorating, handicrafts, dressmaking, diets, novel-writing, flower-arranging, skiing and computers but none of them gave her an inkling of an idea to start a little business. She bought the *Estates Gazette* and spent several hours browsing through it. One item caught her eye. It was an advertisement for a booklet claiming to offer the 'Secrets of Successful Fishing'. It was priced at £5, and the advertiser claimed to have sold many thousands of copies. This intrigued Sally as she was quite sure that there must be hundreds of books on fishing which were probably far more detailed than a mere booklet. She returned to the library to see if any books there offered an opportunity for her to try and write her own booklet.

It was when she went back to the diet section that a thought struck. Although she had read many books on different diets, not one of them had offered a choice. Soon afterwards, Sally sat down to write a collection of diets - they included the Housewife's Diet; the Alcoholic's Diet; The Stone-loss Diet; the Five-Day, Six-Day and Eight-Day Diets, among others. When she had completed her first draft, she sent a photocopy to her solicitor to make sure she had not infringed copyrights. Eventually, at a cost of 75 pence each, she produced *Sally Holmes' Twenty Diets To Happiness*. Through classified columns, baby-wear shops and confectioners, more than 5,000 were sold, giving Sally a profit of more than £6,000 in four months. *Sally Holmes' Twenty Exercises To Happiness* was not so successful, but it did make a profit. *Sally Holmes' Twenty Cocktails Before Bed is* her greatest success so far. For someone with qualifications which did not help her to get a job, Sally is doing very well indeed.

Good-luck story

There is, of course, the real good-luck story of Luigi Pescalli who came to England from Turin utterly penniless. He spoke almost no English. Thirty years later he retired with £500,000 in the bank. Asked on a television programme to explain how he did it, he said, 'I hired a barrow, filled it up with oranges, pushed it from Covent Garden to Oxford Street twice a day and sold my oranges there day after day, month after month, year after year. Then I brought my wife over from Turin, and she had a barrow on the other side of the road. Later, our two sons did the same. We never counted the hours, we never worried about holidays, all we did was work. Then, one day, a no-good uncle who I never see in my life, he died and leave me £500,000.' But that is truly the rare exception.

The sage, Amos Hargraves, once said, 'Cards have taught me a great deal about luck. I do not play cards.'

33

SPOTTING
BUSINESS
IDEAS

Pages 15-21 are largely concerned with becoming more observant. This chapter follows the same line of thought but gives specific examples. They are not all conclusive or even practical for someone about to start in business but are intended, once again, to give readers an approach to recognising new business ideas. Hopefully, other useful possibilities will be spotted as a result.

The major problem with new ideas is to protect oneself from having them stolen. It is impossible to achieve this every time but, on balance, the exercise justifies the effort.

BATHROOM SPECIALISTS Years ago bathrooms were supplied almost exclusively by builders. As house-ownership increased and higher salaries permitted, the bathroom specialist emerged. His showrooms now exhibit a selection of baths, showers, toilets and bidets and the fittings that go with them. Prices range from the modest to the ridiculous. Many people love shops which specialise, and consequently those providing more exclusive bathroom equipment have prospered over recent years. It is surprising that few in this country also keep attractive stocks of towels, flannels, mats, soaps and other bath accessories, and luxuries. Matching colours would surely prove an added attraction for many planning their new bathrooms.

BRIDAL GOWNS It is alleged that in these days of enlightenment when uncouth pop singers carry more influence than parents or priests, young people worry less about getting married or staying married. Unlike the days of old, divorce is easy, commonplace and accepted. Be that as it may, when it comes to the crunch, the average bride wants to marry in white, regardless of whether the marriage takes place in a church or a registrar's office. White still has a certain, often inexplicable, significance which young women associate with the special day in their lives. A white gown represents a clean, wholesome, new life, which the majority want to cherish. Wherever they take place, deep down, most girls still associate weddings with a religious happening, a time for thanksgiving, blessings and goodwill. It follows that buying or hiring a bridal gown is the time when every girl and her mother are likely to feel deeply emotional. Shops who provide these expensive garments could certainly increase their profits by selling Bibles and Prayer Books bound in white leather or leatherette. Even if half the girls find the idea corny and old-fashioned, it still leaves 50 per cent who feel that such a purchase would add something special to the occasion.

LADIES' HAIRDRESSING has become big business. It is no longer considered a great personal indulgence to visit a hairdresser regularly. Unlike hundreds of thousands of women who were happy washing their own hair, their daughters now visit hairdressers. These establishments usually offer a wide selection of cosmetics, and provide tea and magazines for customers who are kept waiting. But what an ideal place to stock ties, greetings cards and paperbacks. If this idea appeals to you, take a walk round your own district, or a richer one if you prefer, and count the number of salons with five chairs or more. There is not a lot of point in concentrating on smaller establishments as such places are unlikely to want to carry much stock. If you believe there is scope in the area of your choice, make notes of the names and addresses of all the hairdressers and then do exactly the same in nearby towns and suburbs. If you can find about fifty, check out with a few whether they would be prepared to allow you to install racks on their premises. Then locate one or two firms who manufacture ties, cards, or whatever other items might occur to you as suitable. Explain that you have a large number of new outlets for their products and enquire whether they would grant you a sales agency. This would be on the strict understanding that you only dealt with firms who were not carrying their stock, and firms within an agreed geographical area. Once you have such an agreement in writing it is then up to you.

DIY FRAMING Today, there are more people than ever who have framed paintings, photographs and prints on their walls. This is evidenced by the increase in the number of shops who now make a good business in this field. Many also stock frames, and quite a number carry DIY framing kits for the customer. Strangely enough, while these kits will often include simple instructions they rarely include such articles as mini-tubes of glue, small nails, eye-screws, or lengths of picture wire. One would think that retailers in this business would find packets of such items of interest. If one could find enough who were, it would not be difficult to build a modest business, albeit as a sideline.

NEWSPAPER SHOPS It is virtually impossible to think of a new product for these shops to carry. The majority already stock magazines, confectionery, smokers' requirements, stationery, small toys, paperback books and odd bits of haberdashery. But they can serve a very useful purpose. Anyone wishing to bring a service or a product to the attention of a captive readership in a given area only has to find a local newsagent prepared to slip an appropriate notice in every newspaper delivered. It usually costs between £1 and £1.50 per 100 and can prove very worthwhile indeed. A practical plan would be to make such arrangements initially with three or four separate newsagents in a given district. Monitoring the written replies or telephone calls should give a clear indication which exercise is worth repeating.

BAKERIES These businesses are mostly concerned with low-priced goods on which profits of pennies are made on each article. Furthermore, there is frequently a wastage element due to unsold goods. The average bakery stocks varieties of bread, rolls, biscuits, cakes and pastries. It would seem logical for them also to include such items as flour, yeast, sugar, raisins, baking tins, and doilies. It could also be a most suitable place for customers to find books on cake-and pastry-baking. The profit margins on these items are substantially higher than on the basic products and there is little chance of any real loss.

FISHMONGERS AND FISH SHOPS At first sight, there would appear to be little opportunity to suggest any additional items for a fish shop. However, there are few that keep a reasonable stock of tinned fish or frying oil. This observation should not lead anyone to believe that such items justify a new business. It does indicate, though, that there are opportunities in unlikely places.

HAT SHOPS Major stores appear to sell the largest number of ladies' hats. But there are still many small shops that provide exclusive designs for those customers who can afford them. Ladies who patronise such boutiques are rarely obliged to give prices greater priority than fashion. The windows of such shops will exhibit as few as half a dozen hats and nothing else. It would seem that they are missing the chance of selling silk scarves and handkerchiefs, and, possibly, beautifully made artificial flowers. The profit margins are good, and such articles are unlikely to become unfashionable.

PHOTOGRAPHERS Professional photographers provide a service largely for people who are celebrating an occasion, a service that must produce many hundreds of thousands of products every year. The best of these invariably finding themselves adorning mantelpieces, desks, pianos and a wide variety of tables. It is surprising that so many of the up-market practitioners in this business do not stock a reasonable selection of photo-frames. The chance to sell them must occur every time a photographer has a customer. Exclusive studios from Bond Street to Knightsbridge, and throughout the country, have instead been providing a highly profitable trade for stores for years. Frames vary in price from around £5 to £200 and offer profit margins between 50 and 100 per cent. Specialising in supplying top photographers would not require a great deal of capital.

HEALTH FOODS The growth of shops specialising in providing health foods has grown enormously in the last ten to twenty years. In the past, one would have to hunt for a little shop tucked away in a back street to find a selection of vegetarian foods and homoeopathic medicines. Today, it is big business with more and more people making determined efforts to stay healthy and live longer. The average age of death is now seven years later than it was thirty years ago; while the National Health Service and a cleaner environment have no doubt been largely responsible for this, few would argue that a greater awareness of healthier diets has also made a considerable contribution to this development. Shops providing these nutritious foods nearly all stock recipe books and literature dealing extensively with health problems which are allegedly solvable. It would therefore seem logical for such shops to stock exercise equipment as a natural aid for greater fitness. Such gear is already proving highly profitable to the larger chemists who stock it — why not health food shops?

WAITING ROOMS The waiting rooms of most professional people are notorious for their dowdy appearance and old copies of magazines. Providing a little cheer and distraction is not often considered part of the service to be offered to patients and clients. This is not always a matter of economics but often due to lack of thought or imagination. Beautifully made artificial flowers are a one-off expense, and can do a great deal to brighten up the waiting rooms of many doctors, dentists, solicitors and others. (See 'Flower Making', page 51.)

Success in concentrated 'spotting' increases with practice. It has probably been responsible for more people recognising new commercial opportunities than any number of business diplomas. As Giorgio Getcelli said, 'No man needs more than one great idea in a lifetime.'

34

WEALTH
WARNINGS

There are asylums for people who attempt DIY brain surgery. Unfortunately, there are still far too many people who endeavour to advise themselves on business matters which they do not understand. By not consulting professionals they often fail to enjoy the many benefits which are available for the self-employed and others in business. Even worse, such people frequently expose themselves to prosecution by assuming an understanding of income tax, Value Added Tax, health regulations, personal and public liabilities, and numerous other matters which require specialist knowledge. It is as well to remember that most inspectors of taxes are highly qualified people blessed with enormous patience and powers of perseverance when it comes to pursuing an errant taxpayer. They also have unlimited time available to do so.

Serious chapters on tax, insurance and pensions are all far too complicated to be included in this book. The reader is well advised to take advice from those qualified to give it, but the following points are simply an indication of matters to be taken seriously.

INCOME TAX Seek the advice of a qualified accountant. He is not just trained to check your tax liability but also to ensure that you enjoy all your tax allowances. In order to avoid any misunderstanding, make quite sure that you are aware of the fees he is going to charge you.

VALUE ADDED TAX Again, take advice from an accountant. He will help you to prepare your figures correctly. Leaving this to chance can cause enormous aggravation, considerable waste of time and unnecessary fees in getting your affairs in order.

INSURANCE If your personal and business insurances are under £250 a year, you are probably best off dealing directly with an

175

insurance company. A qualified, established broker, working on a 10-15 per cent commission can hardly afford to spend much time advising small clients. When choosing an insurance company, go for the well established like Norwich Union, Prudential, Sun Alliance and those organised to cope efficiently with clients of all sizes.

INSURANCE BROKERS Your bank manager or accountant should be able to recommend a broker when you need one. Many banks have insurance departments and they can often be helpful. However, when your business grows, you may well require completely independent advice. Your bank manager should be advising you on banking and financial matters generally. He is rarely an authority on insurance, however hard he may try to convince you to the contrary.

HEALTH REGULATIONS These are particularly important as soon as you have business premises and employees. There are twenty well-staffed offices throughout the country whose prime function is to answer questions concerned with such matters. If in doubt write to: The Health and Safety Executive, Baynards House, Chepstow Place, London W2 4TF (Tel: 071-229 3456).

BANK MANAGER Always keep him well advised of your plans and progress. He is in a position to be helpful, not just with loans but also with introductions. Remember to check all bank charges — they can get out of hand.

START-UP MONEY It is often far too easy to borrow money when one becomes over-enthusiastic about a new business project. Never borrow more than you can comfortably service — that means do not depend on your expectations to pay the interest on your loans. Furthermore, never take a second mortgage on your home for business purposes without discussing it, in detail, with your spouse, your accountant and, if he is not the lender, with your bank manager.

8. PERSONAL INSURANCE Once you start a business it is important to protect your income, or at least part of it, in the event of sickness or accident. Companies like the Norwich Union, Guardian Royal Exchange and Eagle Star are familiar with this essential type of protection.

GAMBLING In principle it is irresponsible to sell one's home to start a business. If one believes that a certain project creates an exception to this rule, do NOT make a decision yourself. Not only should it be discussed with those in 'START-UP MONEY' above but also with several people who are actually in the business. The profits promised by some salesmen can never be realised — be wary of car-wash installations, weighing-machine projects, franchises which you do not understand, businesses dependent on finding the best premises in the right towns, and any offer which requires unknown partners or large stocks for its success.

SMALL IS BEAUTIFUL Many thousands of people can successfully build and operate small profitable businesses. They only run into serious difficulties when they expand too quickly, borrow more than they can afford or take on strangers as partners.

35

GOOD READING

There is rarely need to go any further than a public library to find all the information and data necessary to start a business. The most useful books you will need are usually found in four sections: business, arts and crafts, hobbies, and DIY.

In addition, a visit to your local Citizens' Advice Bureau will ensure that you obtain all the up-to-date information on government grants and allowances.

Do not hesitate to make good use of both establishments — remember, rate-payers and taxpayers provide them for the benefit of all.

It would be impossible and impractical to list all the books which might be interesting to those now stepping out into the business world. The following are just a handful which most readers will find worth owning or browsing through.

Collins English Dictionary or the *Oxford English Dictionary*. Paperback editions can be purchased for around £4.00, or less second-hand. These are absolutely essential for anyone obliged to communicate in writing.

Janner's Complete Letterwriter. Published by Business Books, it is full of good common sense and hundreds of excellent ideas for anyone who has to write letters.

Earning Money At Home. A Consumers' Association Publication with lots of good tips for people wanting to brush up hobbies and skills to money-making standards. Worth reading.

Starting a Small Business by Alan and Deborah Fowler is published by Sphere Money Aids for those with at least £5,000 or more available.

What They Don't Teach You At Harvard Business School by Mark H. McCormack is not an essential book for anyone about to start a small business. But it is interesting and worth browsing through on a wet afternoon.

Starting Your Own Business. A Consumers' Association Publication. Rather a sophisticated book but full of useful addresses of government offices and organisations providing a wide variety of services.

Getting Started, by Robson Rhodes, Chartered Accountants, published by Kogan Page in association with the Institute of Chartered Accountants in England and Wales. This is an all-round basic guide.
Selective Business Writing Skills — A General Guide, by Mielu Rabinovici, Sc. Comm., BA (Soc. Sci.), BEd. This has some useful basic ideas for letter-writing and other business writing skills.
Employment Law for the Small Business, by Anne Knell, published by Kogan Page. This is very useful reading if you are thinking of employing others in your new business.
Blackwells also publish a range of books called *Barclays Guide to ....* such as *The Barclays Guide to Financial Management for the Small Business*, by Peter Wilson. It might be useful to have a look through these books.
How to Promote Your Own Business, by Jim Dudley, published by Kogan Page. This guides you through some ideas for promoting your own business, which can be very useful.

A book only has to give you one good idea to make it worth reading.

Those who feel they would benefit from a seven-day course should communicate with West Dean College, Chichester, West Sussex, P018 OQZ. It offers excellent short courses on a wide range of subjects including glass engraving and furniture polishing.

POSTSCRIPT

If you have read this book and believe it has one idea worth following, take several pieces of paper and a pencil. On the first sheet write your name and your age. Then set out:

The chapters in this book which have interested me most are:

.... Page ....
.... Page ....
.... Page ....

I believe I could start such and such a business because

....

I would take the following steps to get going.

Then make a numbered list of 20 steps and study it carefully. You may well find that the list would be more comprehensive if you made it 30.

If, two days later, that list still looks good to you, get started. Do not wait for any other signals, for the weekend, or for a quieter moment. You have reached the time when, mentally, you are in business. This is the day you have moved from being unemployed to being self-employed.

Good luck.